# DUET FOR T

## A Play in Two Acts

### by

## MARY HAYLEY BELL

**AGAIN FOR**
**JOHNNIE**

SAMUEL FRENCH

### LONDON
#### NEW YORK TORONTO SYDNEY HOLLYWOOD

Basic fee for each and every
performance by amateurs        Code H
in the British Isles

In theatres or halls seating 600 or more the fee will be subject to negotiation.

In territories overseas the fee quoted above may not apply. Application must be made to our local authorized agents, or if there is no such agent, to Samuel French Ltd, London.

Applications to perform the play by professionals should be made to Hughes Massie & Co Ltd, 18 Southampton Place, London WC1.

ISBN 0 573 01116 8

PRINTED IN GREAT BRITAIN
This impression printed by photolithography from the original printing
by W & J Mackay Limited, Chatham

# DUET FOR TWO HANDS

Produced at the Lyric Theatre, London, W.1, on June 27th, 1945, with the following cast of characters:

| | |
|---|---|
| EDWARD SARCLET | *Elwyn Brook-Jones.* |
| HERDA SARCLET | *Elspeth March.* |
| ABIGAIL SARCLET | *Mary Morris.* |
| STEPHEN CASS | *John Mills.* |
| FLETTY | *Merle Tottenham.* |

## SYNOPSIS OF SCENES

### ACT I

SCENE 1.—Forsinard.   An eighteenth-century castle in the Orkney Islands. Midsummer, 1904.   Sunset.

SCENE 2.—The same.   Three hours later.

### ACT II

SCENE 1.—The same.   Next morning.

SCENE 2.—The same.   That night.

SCENE 3.—The same.   Dawn.

# DUET FOR TWO HANDS

## ACT I

### SCENE 1

SCENE.—*Forsinard. An eighteenth-century castle in the Orkneys. Midsummer, 1904. Sunset.*

*The room, which looks across the Bay of Skail to the Atlantic Ocean, has large high windows which lead through a conservatory on to an emerald and beautifully rolled lawn. The room is high and light, the furniture exquisite, with soft carpets and brocades. A wide stone stairway leads up to the floor above, with a stained-glass window at the turn which pours a lilac light down into the room ; below the stairs is an archway leading off to the rest of the house. On the other side of the room is a large Adam fireplace, in front of which are settees and chairs. A large shining grand piano stands alone, down L., the shaft of light from the stairs falling across an enormous bowl of tea roses on it. The roses are the most startling thing about Forsinard ; they are everywhere, the room is full of them, each seems more perfect a bloom than the last, and their heady intoxicating scent fills the room. Here is a bowl of pink, and there another of lemon and again on the mantelshelf, a single scarlet bloom standing alone in a long, thin Chelsea vase under the portrait of a black-browed man in a crimson cloak.*

*(See the Ground Plan and Photograph.)*

*On a small table before the settee, a silver tray with tea and bread and butter stands untouched. There is no sound in the room save for the ticking of the little Spanish clock on the mantel, and the cries of the wheeling kittiwakes as they sail past the windows. A dog barks.*

ABIGAIL SARCLET *enters through the conservatory and into the room. She is a wild, strange-looking girl, and she makes an astonishing picture in her brown full skirt and white blouse with the sleeves rolled up to the elbows, and the sun shining on her black hair and slanting green eyes under their thick fringe of lashes ; round her neck she wears what appears to be a string of rowan berries, and in one hand she carries a rod and fishing basket, in the other her shoes and socks. She walks straight up to the tea-tray, peering at it to see if anyone has had tea. Then she sees a letter addressed to herself which she takes up, at the same time throwing the basket, rod, shoes and socks on the floor at the* L. *end of the settee. She sits on the settee, at the* L. *end, curling herself up on it like a child with her feet under her. She opens the letter and reads.*

5

HERDA SARCLET *enters down the stairs. She has the same dark colouring, the Nordic shape of face and a bearing which is charming and gracious. Her soft hair is swept off her forehead, and when she speaks, it is in an Island voice, which has in it something between Scottish and Welsh.*

HERDA (*coming down the stairs*). Abby! That smelly fish basket on the floor again! (*she crosses to the* L. *end of the settee*)— and your shoes and stockings!—Truly you behave like a—hooligan boy instead of a young lady—— (*She picks up the basket, goes up* C. *into the conservatory and puts it down off* L.)

ABIGAIL (*waving the letter*). I am mistress of five pounds in money!

HERDA. From whom? (*She returns and stands up* C.)

ABIGAIL. I'll read it to you. It's interesting . . . pour me out some tea like a darling. I'm dry as a piece of sacking.

HERDA (*making a face*). What a horribly unattractive simile. (*She comes down to the chair* C., *sits and pours out tea.*) Hadn't you better wash?

ABIGAIL. Heavens no! I've been in the burn the whole day . . . you think too much of washing . . .

(HERDA *hands a cup of tea to* ABIGAIL.)

. . . Shall I read?

HERDA. You haven't told me who it's from. (*She rises and moves up* C.)

ABIGAIL. Now who would send me money? Who would write a three-page letter to the Prisoners of Forsinard from the splendour of his London Town.

HERDA (*turning*). Edward?

ABIGAIL. None other. Edward.

HERDA. You speak as if he owned London——

ABIGAIL. My father owns everything.

HERDA (*coming down to the back of the chair* C.). Oh! What a thing to say.

ABIGAIL. Mind you, I think he's clever. A very, very clever surgeon. I think he's amusing, in his own way. I think he's nice too, sometimes. I'm sorry for him when the medical profession laugh at him and call him names; but I don't respect him; I don't even like him.

HERDA. Abigail!—After sending you five pounds.

ABIGAIL. Och! He'll ask for it back the day after tomorrow. (*She puts her teacup on the tray.*)

HERDA. Naughty—read the letter! (*She moves to the* L. *end of the settee.*)

ABIGAIL. He's bringing someone with him again . . . someone more amusing this time and someone who will make you blush when I say his name!

HERDA. Don't be absurd, child. . . . Who is it your father is bringing ?

ABIGAIL. Guess. (*She holds up three fingers.*)

HERDA. Nonsense.

ABIGAIL. Guess ! Guess !

HERDA. Doctor Canon ?

(ABIGAIL *shakes her head.*)

(*She moves to the side of the chair* C.) Not Mrs. Atkinson ?

ABIGAIL. Someone to make you blush ! Now ! What can Mrs. Atkinson know to make you blush ? Guess again !——

HERDA. There is no one. (*She crosses to* L. *and turns.*) I can think of no one at all.

ABIGAIL. There is. You were reading his book of poems this morning.

(HERDA *stares.*)

HERDA (*moving to* C. ; *wide-eyed*). You mean—you—you don't mean . . . you *can't* mean—— !

ABIGAIL (*settling herself on the settee*). Stephen Cass !

HERDA. Stephen Cass ! (*She turns away, moves a few steps to the* L. *and stops.*) You must be joking, Abby ! Stephen Cass ! Nonsense ! (*She turns and faces* ABIGAIL.)

ABIGAIL. I'll read it to you. Listen. "My dearest daughter, I have long since promised myself a visit to Forsinard and am glad to say that my work now permits, and I shall be with you on the fourteenth——"

HERDA. The fourteenth. That was yesterday ! (*She moves to* C. *and stops.*)

ABIGAIL. "I shall be accompanied by my friend, Stephen Cass, the poet,"

(HERDA *crosses behind the settee to the bookshelves. She picks up a book.*)

"who has been exceedingly ill for two years as the result of that accident at Vogespiegel."

(HERDA *moves to the back of the settee,* L. *end.*)

"He is, however, much himself again and delighted at the prospect of a holiday in the Islands." Don't read over my shoulder, Herdy. "So tell my sister to air linen and prepare a room overlooking the Bay, and I leave it to the two of you to entertain and help him back to strength and health, so that he will become, once again, as one of our more precious reviewers called him, 'The sworn companion of the Wind.'"

HERDA. It was Bertram Lewis said that in the "Blue Magazine." Why does Edward call him "precious" ?

(ABIGAIL *pours out tea.*)

ABIGAIL. Because Edward is not at all precious to anyone.

HERDA. Stephen Cass!—— (*She moves up stage into the conservatory.*) I wonder if he is like his poems ? (*She stands by the pillar between the windows.*)

ABIGAIL (*rising and picking up her fishing-rod*). Which poems ? (*She moves to the fireplace.*) You cannot say of him that he——

HERDA. Ah . . . such mellifluence——

ABIGAIL. I don't read poetry. (*She holds the rod in her hands, looking at it.*)

HERDA (*softly*). You used to—there was a time when you told me " they walked through you." Stephen Cass—I wonder what he's like ! (*She comes down stage and sits in the chair* C.)

ABIGAIL (*shortly*). A nineteenth-century Puck with crumpled linen and a mop of untidy hair. Or worse—a young man of fashion—some masher, perhaps, with languorous affected speech like Edward's Mr. Grevil ! (*She moves below the settee and sits on the bear-skin rug.*)

HERDA. Mr. Grevil was the possessor of the bluest eyes I ever hope to see.

ABIGAIL. Was he ? I found them difficult so see with that fleet of warts on his nose.

HERDA. Abigail ! for a young lady who says——

ABIGAIL. I'm not a young lady !—nor am I an old one, nor yet a child—not even a girl—nor short nor tall nor fat nor thin.

HERDA (*playing with her*). What then ?

ABIGAIL. Oh—I'm nothing . . . nothing . . . (*She plays with the fishing-rod.*)

HERDA (*seriously*). You're everything to me.

(ABIGAIL *rises and moves in front of the settee to the* L. *end.*)

ABIGAIL (*putting the fishing-rod back in its case*). Dear sweet Herdy-Gerdy—thank you ! (*She laughs wickedly.*) What about the room for the Roundeleer ?

(HERDA *rises, crosses up stage to the bookshelves and puts the book back.*)

Edward said the fourteenth—it's the fifteenth and the packet from Thurso arrives at two—at Stromness. . . . They ought to be here before supper.

(HERDA *comes behind the* L. *end of the settee, picks up the socks and crosses to the stairs.*)

HERDA (*excitedly*). What an enthralling supper ! Fancy ! Stephen Cass at Forsinard ! (*She starts up the stairs.*)

ABIGAIL. You said that as you might have said—Fancy God on the Skerries !

HERDA (*turning*). Mind your words, Abigail Sarclet !

ABIGAIL (*going up stage into the conservatory with the rod*).

Wear your brown cambric muslin tonight, it sets off your eyes and hair. (*She puts down the rod in the conservatory, out of sight* L. *of the window.*)

HERDA. Oh, shall I ? I thought perhaps my black——

ABIGAIL (*returning and coming down* C. ; *with a sudden change of tone*). It is I who should wear that colour.

HERDA. Abby !—I wish—oh, I do wish——

ABIGAIL (*sternly*). What do you wish ? (*She crosses below the tea-table to the fireplace, and turns.*)

HERDA (*making a gesture of helplessness*). You are such a strange mixture of bitterness and—and—joy and youth and extreme old age ! (*She comes quickly down the stairs and crosses to* ABIGAIL, *laughing suddenly.*) You really are quite a handful to live with, my darling, although I wouldn't be away from you for a moment ! But truly, when I wake in the morning I don't know who I'm going to meet for breakfast !—a haughty young lady, a schoolgirl in a ragged blouse with her hair chopped off with a penknife, or just a crofter's boy. (*She turns and crosses* L. *She starts up the stairs.*)

ABIGAIL (*smiling*). You can always be sure about the crofter's boy !—— Perhaps I'll away with my hair altogether so I can pull my forelock to you, as I do in my heart.

HERDA (*on the landing ; smiling*). And what shall you wear tonight ?—the pretty yellow cloud from Bath is perfect.

ABIGAIL. I'm not changing.

HERDA. What !

ABIGAIL. I've washed my neck, it should be enough for a poet. (*She turns to the fireplace.*)

HERDA. Abby ! Gracious me ! Look at the time. (*She runs down the stairs to the archway at* L. *and calls :*) Fletty ! Fletty !

(*She runs up the stairs and off.* ABIGAIL *turns. A very little old mouse of a grey woman appears in the archway. She looks at* ABIGAIL *in a questioning manner, chewing hard on a piece of crust all the time.*)

ABIGAIL (*crossing and kneeling on the chair* C.). Mr. Edward is arriving in three and a half minutes from England.

FLETTY (*starting up the stairs*). Och !—he's the de'il himsel'—— (*She stops on the landing.*)

ABIGAIL. He is bringing a friend. Mr. Stephen Cass. He is a poet, Fletty.

FLETTY. Och, I ken him.

ABIGAIL. You can't ken him, he's a new friend of Mr. Edward's.

FLETTY. Der ne fule lek an ald fule and da stillest watter breeds da warst wirm.

ABIGAIL. You never listen to anything anyone says, you just

answer yourself; one fine day you'll set yourself a problem and then you'll be getting yourself into trouble with your answer.

FLETTY (*unmoved*). Miss Herda——

ABIGAIL. In the Bay room changing the linen.

FLETTY. Och! You were an ugly baby too——

(*She disappears up the stairs at a speed surprising in one of her size and age. She is a mouse, she looks like a mouse and she moves like a mouse. ABIGAIL gets off the chair and moves to the fireplace. She leans over the rose on the mantel, touching it with gentle fingers.*)

ABIGAIL. Why are you so beautiful?

(*She looks up suddenly, hearing voices and the sound of a wagon. Then, seizing her skirts, she tears up the stairs. The voices are getting nearer now; men's voices, talking. Then two figures enter the conservatory and come up to the window. SARCLET is the first. He strides through the window and into the room, a fat thin tall short man of strange magnetic personality. He is wearing an overcoat and carries a black bag. He strides forward like a man proud of his home and glad to be back. He walks to the middle of the room, putting the black bag on the serving-table as he passes.*)

SARCLET (*turning back to the window*). Come in, Stephen, come in! (*He crosses L. to the archway, and calls.*) Abigail! Herda! —we've arrived.

(STEPHEN CASS *steps into the room, looking about him with keen, interested eyes. He is a slender young man, dark and striking, almost entirely enveloped in an Inverness cape. His face is pale and his hair blown by the wind; only his eyes, flashing from his face like bits of cyprian-blue glass, show any colour. He comes C. and stands still. SARCLET returns to C. and gently removes the cape from his shoulders. Underneath he wears a Norfolk jacket; and below the sleeve ends, his two hands, encased in white gloves, hang by his side.*)

(*Eagerly.*) Well, what do you think of it? (*He puts the cape on the stair rail, takes off his own coat and puts it on top.*)

(CASS *stands smiling, looking about, noting everything.*)

CASS. It's beautiful, Edward—beautiful. I had no idea the Orkneys could have such peace.

SARCLET. They're like women, my dear fellow—change in an instant—tomorrow may be wild, wet and wintry. Tea! (*He comes down to the table and sits in the chair* C.) What could be more expedient! Not the hottest of tea, and cups already used, but better to have this than wait three hours for Fletty to bring us some more.

Cass (*moving to the piano*). Roses ! Roses in the Orkneys ?
(*He turns to* Sarclet.)

Sarclet. Rather special ones too. Abigail's work when she
bothers. She has what the gardeners call " the green thumb of
the earth." (*He pours out two cups of tea.*)

(Cass *runs up the stairs and looks out of the window.*)

Cass. " Here all the summer of my life I'll stay." You
should be a painter, Edward, and live here always.

Sarclet. Why ?

Cass. Then you would be rich enough to buy immortality.

Sarclet. If I had immortality I would sell it. Now come
and have some tea and then I'll show you round.

(Cass *moves down and crosses to the fireplace. He turns and faces*
Sarclet.)

Cass. Edward, I do love this place.

Sarclet. It will do you the world of good. Come along now,
sit down.

(Cass *sits in the middle of the settee.*)

You look quite white. You get very over-excited nowadays,
don't you ?

Cass. Do I, Edward ? (*He takes out his handkerchief and
folds it between his fingers and the teacup.*)

Sarclet. Still afraid of hot things ?

Cass. A bit. (*He lifts the cup carefully.*)

Sarclet. Put some cold milk into it.

Cass (*sipping it*). It's all right.

(Sarclet *watches* Cass *put the cup down.*)

Sarclet. Excellent. I notice you hardly ever knock anything over now.

Cass. Oh, I'm progressing, Doctor ! You'll be surprised !
Don't forget, it's—what ?—five weeks now since you saw them.

Sarclet. Much healthier . . . extraordinarily strong nerve
ends for eighteen months . . . any trouble round the scar now ?

Cass. Everything clear. Doctor Roberts said I needn't wear
gloves, but——

Sarclet. But you like wearing them, don't you ?

Cass. I have a theory.

Sarclet. What's that ?

Cass. . . . I don't want anyone to see them yet . . .

Sarclet. You speak as if they were unsightly—or something.

Cass. It's all right when I look down and see them, they look
perfectly ordinary, just like anyone else's hands . . . but if I'm
not looking at them—sometimes they feel—heavy and ugly and
full of blood. . . . When the gloves are on—I feel—more easy !
More confident !

SARCLET  Nonsense!  Imagination.

(CASS *looks round.*)

CASS.  Edward, do they know about me ?—Do they know what to expect ?

SARCLET.  Not yet.  But does that matter ?

CASS.  It's—it's shaking hands . . . taking hold of things—I'm so clumsy at times . . .  They'll think I have some strange tumour on the brain, or that I'm a drunkard like you——

SARCLET.  You must just be an old gallant, and bow deeply.

CASS.  That's what I usually do, but it nearly always ends in confusion.

SARCLET.  I shall tell them.  We shall both tell them—they will be overwhelmed by our prowess.

CASS.  Perhaps they'll be horrified and ask me to go.

SARCLET.  What ?—at the most exciting operation that's been performed ?  My dear fellow, you are talking to doctor's women.

CASS.  Where are they ?  I want to meet them.

SARCLET.  Changing, no doubt.  I tell you it's a great event, bringing up a distinguished lion of a poet——

CASS (*rising and going to the fireplace*).  Who has produced nothing for two years !  (*He stands with his back to* SARCLET.) I'm not a poet, Edward—I'm a specimen of surgery.

SARCLET.  Abigail will inspire you !  She's the oddest child you ever met—did I say child ?

(CASS *looks at a miniature at the downstage end of the mantelpiece. He points to it.*)

CASS (*looking closer at it*).  Is this her ?

SARCLET.  No, no, that's her mother.

CASS.  Wonderful face.

SARCLET.  A fish constantly out of water—a cat always on the wrong side of the door.  When Abigail was born I dare not look at her for years.

CASS.  What were you afraid of ?

SARCLET.  What I should see—fish, fowl or fur——

CASS.  And when you looked ?  (*He turns to him.*)  What did you see ?

(SARCLET *frowns.*)

SARCLET (*quietly*).  A little girl with black hair sitting on a blue chair—but she isn't like that any more—she's like me now —except that I walk alone in the city——  (*He looks up at the picture over the fireplace.*)

CASS (*suddenly*).  Is that you there in fancy dress ?

SARCLET.  That's my grandfather.

CASS.  Oh, the Spanish pirate—the Romney.

SARCLET. I'm rather proud of that picture. I look at it and say " You were a pirate on the Spanish main, and I am a successful surgeon. What do you think of me ? "

CASS. And does the ceiling fall ? (*He comes down* R.)

SARCLET. You have no respect, Cassius, for your saviour.

CASS (*turning to* SARCLET). I think you're rating it a bit high at that. As a matter of fact I have enormous respect for you, but I like pulling your leg when you become pompous. Tell me some more.

SARCLET (*sulkily*). What more ?

CASS (*laughing, and going up to the table in front of* SARCLET). Now you're angry because your grandfather and I are not on our knees.

SARCLET. No. I'm never angry . . . I'm the most equable of men.

CASS (*turning to the settee*). And your sister . . . what of her ? (*He sits.*)

SARCLET. A change of life child. Should be brilliant, like me —but contrives only to be a good housekeeper.

CASS. If hers is the vibration of this house I would call her more than a good housekeeper, I would say of her that she was charming and witty and gay and that she had a deep quiet laugh——

SARCLET. The vibration is pure Sarclet. The blend of Spanish and Nordic—the quiet of the hills—the violence of the sea . . . the winds in winter . . . and just time waiting——

CASS. Waiting for what ?

SARCLET. Everyone is waiting for something—Success—Love —Happiness—Children. Life is waiting—isn't it ?

CASS. Life is opportunity. . . . But for which of these is Edward Sarclet waiting ?

(SARCLET *laughs and waves him away with a gesture of his long-fingered hand.*)

SARCLET. It's not children ! (*He rises and moves up to the serving-table.*) But it's all the rest, they seem wrapped together and I never had any of them. But you mock me, Cassius ! . . . That is an Adam mantelpiece. (*He picks up a decanter.*)

CASS. Yes . . . it's charming.

SARCLET. My grandfather brought it from Edinburgh. Whisky, Stephen ? (*He pours out a drink.*)

CASS. No, I don't think so. (*He pauses.*) Edward, tell me, was he a very nervy person ?

SARCLET. Who, my grandfather ? (*He comes down to the* L *arm of the settee with his drink.*)

CASS. No. (*He lifts his* L. *hand towards* SARCLET.) He——

SARCLET. How should I know ? Why should you suppose that ?

CASS. I'm not supposing. I'm trying to find out!

SARCLET. You're always trying to find out, aren't you? (*He crosses to the armchair* C.) And I keep telling you, I know no more. (*He sits.*)

CASS. I never can understand why you'll tell me nothing about him. It stands to reason that I must be intrigued . . . more than intrigued, fascinated—obsessed . . .

SARCLET. You mustn't be obsessed. You won't always feel like that. As the hands get more mobile, and you get less pain attacks, you'll forget about—that . . . you'll just take them for granted, like the rest of us do. You'll move through life, forgetting more and more every day.

CASS. No. I shall never do that. (*He leans forward.*) Waking or sleeping, he is a very definite individual. Trying to make himself known to me. . . . In some ways he has succeeded already——

SARCLET (*angrily*). Sentimental rot! He wasn't a definite individual at all. He was just a man. Just a rolling stone. (*He drinks.*)

CASS. No one is " just a man "—or " just a woman." (*He sits back.*) He must have been a singular individual. I want to know more about him. Some day I shall. Some day I shall find the missing pieces of the puzzle—every day, everywhere I go—I'm on the watch for it—crossing the park by the Serpentine, pausing by a doorway, entering a room, p'raps it's there!-- p'raps it's here!

SARCLET (*turning to* CASS). Are you sure what you're looking for ?

CASS. When I find it I shall be.

SARCLET (*rising and crossing up* L. *abruptly*). Where are those girls ? (*He walks up to the foot of the stairs, looking up. Then, without turning, he speaks casually.*) What do you mean, when you say he tries to make himself known to you ? (*He turns.*) How can such a thing be ?

CASS (*delighted*). You see, in spite of yourself you are interested.

SARCLET. Naturally I'm interested, Cassius. You forget I'm the perpetrator of the offending articles, such an operation has never been performed before, naturally I'm interested in all its facets. (*He moves to* C.)

CASS. Of course, but you must admit that there was a time, early on, when I could never get you to discuss two words about the offending articles.

(SARCLET *crosses to the settee and leans over the* L. *arm.*)

SARCLET. That was for your own sake. I wanted you to try and think of them as your own hands, your own hands which had suffered an accident and were in plaster, and from which you had

pain.  I wanted you to think day by day, night by night—that—
way——

CASS.  But I've told you before, that way was never possible.
Whoever they belonged to in that "other life" was a man of
great strength, both physically and in character.  I'm sure of
that.

(SARCLET *moves to the serving-table.*)

SARCLET.  What makes you say so ?  How can you possibly
say so ?  (*He puts down his empty glass.*)

CASS.  Different things.  (*He looks at* SARCLET.)

SARCLET.  Tell me.  (*He turns down stage and moves to the
back of the chair* C.)

CASS.  Why don't *you* tell *me* ?

SARCLET (*leaning on the back of the chair*).  There's nothing I
can tell you.

CASS.  You didn't know him ?

(SARCLET *shakes his head.*)

But you saw him.  Well, what did he look like then ?

SARCLET.  He was dead, Cassius.

CASS.  Well ?  (*He rises and moves up to* SARCLET *by the
R. arm of the chair.*)  Was he big or small, heavy or light ?  Was
his hair brown or fair and his eyes——?

SARCLET.  A dead man isn't anyone (*he pauses*) . . . and
anyway I don't like getting into medical talk of that kind.  (*He
crosses down* R. *and sits in the armchair.*)

CASS (*laughing*).  I understand, Edward, I (*he moves round the
table to the front of* SARCLET)—understand, but you've done
something, you know ; giving me the hands of a man you didn't
know.

SARCLET.  What do you mean ?

CASS (*laughing*).  Well, he might have been anyone—a king
or a murderer !  (*He stands facing* SARCLET.)

(SARCLET *stares at him.*)

SARCLET (*slowly*).  But even supposing he had been *–that* . . .
it couldn't affect you.  You have a man's *hands*, not his brain.

(CASS *leans over* SARCLET.)

CASS.  But the *habits* . . .

SARCLET.  No, Cassius . . .

CASS (*persisting*).  . . . the addictiveness must go on, and in
time as things grow stronger habit becomes power, therefore I
contend sometimes I am under another man's authority.

SARCLET.  Each man has his own development from childhood
—your hands follow *your* brain, not his.

(CASS *straightens up and turns away from* SARCLET.)

CASS (*crossing to the piano*). I know all that, but there is something else. (*He is looking at the roses.*) "More things in heaven and earth, Horatio——"

SARCLET. Rot ! . . . Rot, Cassius, rot !

CASS (*sitting on the piano-stool*). Well, Doctor, supposing it was his eye ? Supposing he was colour-blind ? I should be colour-blind in that eye too.

SARCLET. It would in any case be impossible to prove because colour is unprovable. What you and I have learnt to call green may——

CASS. Don't quibble !

SARCLET. Well, don't sentimentalize over this man.

CASS. So you don't believe my hands are under any mastery ? You refuse to listen to any of my experiences——

SARCLET. Certainly not ! I'm prepared to listen, but I refuse to believe such arrant nonsense.

CASS (*quietly*). They are, you know.

SARCLET. One day I'm going to do something else . . . something they laugh at me for now. I'm going to make a completely new face, bone structure—everything—— Under your theory that should give a man a new personality and character, but it won't.

CASS. It will. The shock of such a thing alone will change a man. (*He looks at* SARCLET *with an admiring smile.*)

SARCLET (*leaning forward*). I say it won't. It will be the greatest thing in surgery—skin grafting, bone grafting.

CASS. I hope I live to see it.

SARCLET. Then you'll live to eat your words.

(CASS *rises.*)

CASS (*moving up* C.). We're all at your mercy ! It's terrifying how we're all in the hands of surgeons and doctors ! (*He turns down stage between the settee and the chair* C.) None of us knows anything about our bodies, and directly we get ill we're at the mercy of (*he looks at* SARCLET)—indifferent strangers !

SARCLET. Now what d'you mean ? I call those hard and ungrateful words !

(CASS *moves to* SARCLET *and stands in front of him.*)

CASS. Well, aren't we ? I used to lie in bed at that hospital and watch people, like children going in varying stages of emotion to the operating theatre . . . and I used to think what great humanitarians the medical profession had to be. And how easy, too, it would be—to—destroy life instead of to save it.

SARCLET (*dryly*). You don't have to be a surgeon to destroy life.

CASS. But look how easy it is for you, Edward ! The law puts implements of death into your hands.

SARCLET. You don't give the benefit of anything to our brains, I notice. They wouldn't *be* implements of death if we didn't know how to use them ! And the Law, as you put it, is just as stringent with us as it is with anyone else.

CASS (*leaning over* SARCLET). No, because you get the benefit of the doubt ! Because you all cling together, swearing black is white and white is black if necessary—even in death——

SARCLET. You haven't answered my first question yet. How does the previous owner of the hands make himself known to you, as you put it ?

CASS. There you are, you see—you are an accessory after the fact !

SARCLET (*looking round*). What nonsense you do talk—for a poet——

CASS (*turning away and crossing towards the stairs*). That is our prerogative.

SARCLET. Well, I'm still waiting.

CASS (*stopping* c. ; *suddenly serious*). It's hard to explain all of a sudden like this . . . it's . . . *strange* . . . he makes himself known to me in a lot of different ways, some little, some big——

SARCLET (*watching him*). Such as ?

CASS (*standing* c.). Places I've never been to, things are familiar to the touch. Things I have never known, places never seen, and in these last weeks I've had the idea that I should expect to find him . . . repay him in some way ! I find myself on the look-out—almost as though I expected him to pull my sleeve and point the way——

SARCLET (*rising*). He'll be pointing the way to an asylum if you talk like that.

(CASS *moves down to the piano-stool.* ABIGAIL *appears at the top of the stairs.*)

ABIGAIL. Hullo ! Father !

(CASS *turns : he and* SARCLET *look up suddenly to the top of the stairs, and see the girl in her yellow cloud frock from Bath. She smiles down over the stairs and comes slowly down, her eyes on* CASS, *her head a little on one side—then she puts out her two hands to* SARCLET.)

SARCLET (*going to her at the foot of the stairs*). Abby——
ABIGAIL. Hullo ! Hullo !
SARCLET. This is Stephen Cass, Abigail.

(ABIGAIL *holds out her hand with an enigmatic smile of recognition, noting at once everything about him, the pale face and the wing of dark hair falling back off his forehead.* STEPHEN CASS *smiles back. He goes up to her and takes her hand. She notes the slim white gloves.*)

CASS. But I know you quite well.

ABIGAIL. I know you too.

SARCLET. See, Cassius ? How your poetry travels !

CASS (*looking at* ABIGAIL ; *still holding her hand*). You don't mean that, do you ? We've met before, Edward. How nice to see you again.

SARCLET. Nonsense.

CASS. Where was it ? London ? Brussels ? Scheidegg in the mountains ?

ABIGAIL (*smiling and shaking her head*). I've never been there. It was here.

CASS. I've never been here !

SARCLET (*turning away*). Really, you two ! (*He comes to down* C.) It was New Year's Eve, and it was me ! (*He turns back to them.*) She's never left the Islands, you've never been to them ! What are you talking about ? I apologize for both of you !

(CASS *continues to look at* ABIGAIL. *She crosses him and comes down to* SARCLET.)

I must warn you, Cassius, that Island children have no inhibitions, they say anything . . . anything !

(CASS *follows* ABIGAIL *down and stands to* L. *of her. She turns towards him and they face each other, shy suddenly, like children.*)

ABIGAIL (*smiling at him*). Sit down, please, I was forgetting —you must be tired after your long journey.

CASS. No, I'm not, really.

ABIGAIL. Some tea, perhaps ?

SARCLET. We've already had what was left of yours. All we need now is a wash, a change and a spring tide of whisky. Where is Herda ?

ABIGAIL. She won't be long. (*To* CASS.) My aunt is much excited by your visit. She has read all your poems.

CASS (*smiling*). Have you read them ?

ABIGAIL. Yes——

SARCLET. I don't understand half of them——

CASS. Nor do I !

SARCLET (*suddenly turning away and crossing to the armchair down* R.). You will be delighted to hear that Stephen was much taken with our Old Man of Hoy, (*he sits*) he'll probably write something about him that nobody understands too.

CASS (*moving up to the conservatory*). Can we see him from here ? (*He pauses by the pillar, looking out.*)

ABIGAIL (*moving down stage round the tea-table to the settee ; watching* CASS). Unfortunately no, we face the Atlantic. But we can pay him a visit, can't we, Father ?

SARCLET. I warn you, Cassius, they believe in him like mad,

and make arduous pilgrimages to something called the Dwarfies
Cave !

(CASS *moves up into the conservatory.*)

ABIGAIL (*moving up* R. *of the settee*). It's a terrible place. The
sun never gets there. (*She moves up to the window.*) There is
supposed to be a buried village just past that wall—Skerra Brea.
(*She stands half in the conservatory, her back to the pillar.*)

CASS (*not looking round*). Oh yes ! The megalithic village.

ABIGAIL. That will interest you, I know.

CASS. Oh yes, I'm sure it will. (*He indicates something in the
distance.*) What are those Standing Stones ? Are they tomb-
stones ? (*He turns to* ABIGAIL.) What is their significance ?

SARCLET. Something about the persistence of the soul after
death. (*With a sly smile.*) What we were arguing about before
Abby arrived.

ABIGAIL (*to* CASS). Don't tell me that you don't believe in the
persistence of the soul after death ?

SARCLET. It's I who don't believe. Cass believes that there
are more things in heaven and earth than are dreamt of in our
philosophy . . .

ABIGAIL. You couldn't live here and not believe that . . . I
hope that Islands like you !

CASS. So do I.

(*Again they find themselves staring at each other.* CASS *turns
towards* SARCLET *with a smile and catches sight of the rose in
its singular position on the mantelshelf.*)

(*To* SARCLET.) I must congratulate you on the roses. I believe
it is quite a triumph growing them up here. That lonely cne
on the mantelshelf is excellent.

SARCLET. The Old Man of Hoy must have prompted that
remark.

ABIGAIL (*coming down to the fireplace ; delighted*). That's
mine ! I bred it ! I grafted it ! It's unique—— (*She takes
the vase down from the mantelpiece.*)

CASS. Has it a name ? (*He follows her down.*)

ABIGAIL (*turning to him*). It's called the " Vendetta." (*She
takes the rose out of the vase.*)

SARCLET (*surprised ; turning to them and laughing*). My father
was a great authority on roses ; I swear he liked them better
than he liked any of us !

(ABIGAIL *sniffs the rose ; then, almost without realizing what she
is doing, she puts it into* CASS's *hand.*)

ABIGAIL. It's for you.

CASS. No ! It should stay in water, it's too perfect to die.
(*He takes the rose in his hand.*)

SARCLET. Put it behind your ear, my dear fellow !

ABIGAIL (*with a hint of bitterness*). Everything has to die some time.

(HERDA *enters down the stairs. She stands for a second on the half-landing.*)

HERDA. Edward! (*She comes down the remaining steps.*)
SARCLET (*rising*). Herda . . . my sister—Stephen Cass.

(ABIGAIL *puts back the vase on the mantelshelf.* CASS *turns above the* R. *end of the settee towards the stairs. He finds himself face to face with a woman in the early thirties with an oddly attractive crooked smile and* EDWARD'S *yellow-brown eyes and soft brown hair.* CASS *crosses up* C., *holding out his hand.* HERDA *moves to meet him and, after a second's hesitation, takes his hand.*)

HERDA. We are so proud and delighted to see you here.
CASS. How charming of you, Miss Sarclet, I have been looking forward to it.
HERDA. Will I get you some tea, or some whisky after the journey?

(*She comes down* L. *of the chair* C. CASS *follows down between the chair and the settee.*)

CASS. No, thank you.
HERDA. Please sit down. (*She sits in the chair* C.) Edward tells us that you have been ill. I am so sorry.
CASS. Yes, but I'm well again now. (*He sits on the settee.*)
HERDA (*with a glance at* ABIGAIL). Abby!

(ABIGAIL *sits on the fire-stool.*)

Edward!

(SARCLET *looks at* HERDA *and then sits in the armchair down* R.)

This is a splendid place. I'm sure our strange Orkney winds will blow away the rest of your ill health.
CASS. Yes—er—Edward looks a little pale, don't you think?
HERDA. Yes, indeed, Edward looks in need of a holiday. How are you, my dear Edward?
SARCLET. If you mean that Edward looks green it is because of what your strange Orkney winds did to the packet.
HERDA. Oh, that sea! How dangerous it can be!
CASS. When did you last cross to Scotland, Miss Herda?
HERDA. Ah!—It must be almost ten years ago!—We were on a visit to Edinburgh. I remember I wore a plaid travelling cloak and everyone——

(SARCLET *leans forward in his chair.*)

SARCLET (*interrupting*). I feel certain, Herda, that Stephen would like to be taken to his room.
HERDA. But, of course. (*She rises.*) Fletty has put some

warm water there for you, and your traps are already up. (*She crosses to the stairs.*)

> (CASS *rises and moves to the* L. *end of the settee.*)

I'll show you the way. I do hope the journey wasn't too much for you.

CASS (*crossing to the stairs*). No—I enjoyed every moment of it.

> (HERDA *starts up the stairs.* CASS *follows her.*)

HERDA. Have you been to the Islands before, Mr. Cass ?

> (*He hesitates on the stairs and looks back at* ABIGAIL. *She rises.* CASS *follows* HERDA *on up.*)

CASS. No, never. Invergordon is my farthest point north till now. (*He pauses.*) I shall be able to say I have almost reached the land of the midnight sun !

> (HERDA *and* CASS *go off. Their voices die away along the landing.* ABIGAIL *stands watching them, her hands folded at her heart.* SARCLET *turns to her.*)

SARCLET. What do you think of him ?

ABIGAIL. I like him . . . but then I always liked him.

SARCLET. Impossible ! How can you ? You've never met before.

ABIGAIL. Oh—but yes——

SARCLET. How ? Where ? When could you have met him ? (*He rises.*)

ABIGAIL. He knows me too.

> (SARCLET *crosses to down* C. *He laughs, throwing back his head in a familiar gesture.*)

SARCLET. You Island women ! (*He puts his* R. *hand in his jacket pocket.*) Look what I have for a beautiful girl !

> (*He takes out a blue velvet case, snapping it open. He turns to her. Inside lies a moonstone and pearl pendant.* ABIGAIL *runs down to him.*)

ABIGAIL. Oh, what a lovely thing—pearls and moonstones.

SARCLET. Tears and moonlight . . .

ABIGAIL. Tears ?

SARCLET. Pearls for tears, they say—ridiculous. Your mother's favourite stones. Let me fasten it.

> (ABIGAIL *turns her back.* SARCLET *fastens the chain round her neck. She turns to face him. He steps back towards* L. *and looks at her.*)

Beautiful . . . so like your mother sometimes—the same elegance, the same lift of the head, and you have a way of standing that she had, a slight swaying of the body that was most wicked . . . that seemed to know so much and say so preposterously little.

ABIGAIL. "Are *you* wicked, Edward? Are you as wicked as you look?"

(*For a second he is startled, then* ABIGAIL *laughs, and relieved, he does too.*)

SARCLET. That was exactly like her! You cheeky puss!

(*He holds out his hand and draws her to him. He turns and puts his* L. *arm round her shoulders. They move towards the piano.*)

Come, tell me what you have been doing while I slaved away in the south for you.

ABIGAIL. You tell me what you have been doing. I'm sure that will be a great deal more amusing, for we have just ridden, or walked in the seaweed with no shoes on. What have you been doing?

SARCLET. Working, working, working! I'm glad you like Stephen, he is much lionized by tittering London hostesses, and yet you must admit he is unaffected.

(*They continue in a sweep up* R. *to the foot of the stairs.*)

ABIGAIL. Why does he wear white gloves? Is that some new London fashion?

SARCLET. He has had an operation performed on his hands.

ABIGAIL. What sort of operation? Did you perform it?

SARCLET. Yes.

ABIGAIL. What did you do?

(*They stop by the foot of the stairs; facing down stage.*)

SARCLET (*suddenly excited*). Abby, (*he turns to face her and seizes both her hands*) I am so intoxicated by the success of this operation that I must tell you, though strictly speaking it is still a secret and few people know about it, nobody outside the profession!

(ABIGAIL *waits for him to go on.*)

Let me see, where shall I begin? He had an accident . . . (*He releases* ABIGAIL.) . . . Oh, I need not go into details . . . his hands, they had to be amputated . . .

(ABIGAIL *sits* C. *on the bottom stair.*)

There was nothing unusual about that, hundreds of soldiers in the South African War had amputations . . . (*he stands over* ABIGAIL, *by the* R. *side of the stairs*) but the difference is . . . that Stephen has got new hands.

(ABIGAIL *doesn't understand.*)

(*Excitedly.*) I performed a most intricate operation, Abby! Nobody, nobody had ever attempted it, and nobody would believe it could be any good . . . but it was! It was! One hundred per cent good!

ABIGAIL.   What was it?

SARCLET.   I took the hands off a man and I put them on to Stephen Cass!

(ABIGAIL *puts her hands to her mouth in a sudden gesture.*)

ABIGAIL (*horrified*).   But—what—what about the man you took them from?

SARCLET.   He was dead, you silly child! He was dead!

ABIGAIL.   Oh!

SARCLET.   It was this—something like this—that I had been waiting for, something to show the scoffers, the medical profession. " Scarlet "—they called me, but they'll use another name when this month's " Lancet " comes out, they'll be bowing the knee and scraping the ground—and there'll be more, too—men and women with desperate faces—asking for Sarclet, the great surgeon, to operate on them——

ABIGAIL.   It's like a nightmare.

SARCLET.   A nightmare! What's more horrible about it than any other operation? There'll be stranger and more marvellous operations performed, Abby, before you are an old lady, transfusions and graftings such as these miserable acidosis octogenarians could never begin to comprehend . . . such as only I believe in.

ABIGAIL.   But that other man—how——?

SARCLET.   He was dead, I tell you! Leave him alone, you're as bad as Stephen, always probing and poking and asking questions about the wretched man. (*He turns away from her and moves down towards the armchair down* R.)

ABIGAIL.   If I were Stephen I should never rest content till I knew. Never. Never. Never . . .

SARCLET.   Abby, I'm disappointed in you. This wonderful achievement, and not one word of congratulation.

ABIGAIL (*jumping up and following him down to below the tea-table*).   But, oh, of course I do congratulate you, Father, it's—it's just—difficult to stop thinking about it—it would be enough, surely—to send a man demented.

SARCLET (*turning by the armchair; sharply*).   Why? (*He goes to her.*)

ABIGAIL.   That other man's hands—what kind of hands are they? Where did they live? What did they do? Why, he might shake hands with that man's wife and—(*her voice rises*) she would know the feel of his hands and die! (*She catches her breath sharply, holding on to it without letting it out.*)

(SARCLET *shakes her.*)

SARCLET. Stop it ! You'll work yourself up into one of your fits of hysteria if you go on like that. I wish I had never told you now, silly child—and for goodness' sake don't tell Herda. I don't want her muling and puking round me.

(ABIGAIL *doesn't answer.*)

Come on, I had better go up and change. (*He puts his* R. *arm round her shoulders.*) Come with me and tell me about this lawn tennis.

(SARCLET, *up stage of* ABIGAIL, *leads her towards the stairs.*)

Mr. Grevil told me all about you——

(*They start up the stairs.*)

—and how you got angry and hit him with your bat !

(ABIGAIL *still doesn't answer.*)

But he was a silly man—and I should have done the same ! Though in your case he found you the more intriguing, while I should have been run in for assault and battery !

(*They disappear round the bend of the stairs,* SARCLET'S *voice fading off in the distance.*
*The kittiwakes wheel and wail past the window.*
*The little old mouse called* FLETTY *enters through the archway. She starts to cross to the tea-table but notices that the whisky decanter, on the serving-table, is empty. She goes up* C., *picks up the decanter, and goes out with it through the archway.* HERDA *enters down the stairs. At the same moment* FLETTY *enters through the archway with a full decanter. She crosses to the serving-table and puts the decanter down.* HERDA *comes down the stairs and moves to the chair* C.)

HERDA. Did you see Mr. Edward, Fletty ? (*She turns up to* FLETTY *and notices the coats on the stair-rail.*)

FLETTY (*coming down between the settee and the chair to the tea-table*). I ken he's here. (*She comes downstage of the table and takes up the tray.*)

HERDA (*going up to the stairs*). He looks tired, but then he has been working hard. (*She takes the coats off the rail.*)

FLETTY. Butter wouldna melt in his muth—— (*She starts towards the door.*)

HERDA (*coming down to* FLETTY *at* C.). And Mr. Cass, what a charming gentleman ! (*She puts the two coats over* FLETTY'S *arm.*)

FLETTY. Every one to his taste, as Robbie said when he kissed da ku——

(FLETTY *goes out through the archway.* HERDA *moves the tea-table to* L. *of the chair* C., *then goes up to the serving-table for the bowl of roses. She brings them down and sets them on the tea-table, then goes up again to the serving-table. She takes the black bag to the bookcase in the corner up* R. *and returns once more to the serving-table. She brings the cigarette-box down to the tea-table, and then continues down* R. *to the work-table. She takes out some work and sits in the armchair down* R. CASS *enters down the stairs. He has changed into a dark coat. He smiles at* HERDA *from the half-landing. Then he comes down three steps.*)

HERDA. You feel more refreshed now, I'm sure.

CASS. I feel wonderfully refreshed ! I'm looking forward to seeing your beautiful Islands. (*He leans on the stair-rail.*) I have long had the wish to come here.

HERDA (*simply*). If you love them, there isn't anything quite like them anywhere—at least not to me.

CASS. I think that applies to anywhere or anything one loves. I feel the same about Switzerland—and yet I believe far in the north of China——

HERDA. Oh, have you ever been to China ?

CASS. No . . . (*He rubs his thumbs against his fingers as though he were feeling something.*)

HERDA. We had a friend who went to China, he had travelled everywhere, and yet he was always happy to come back to the Orkneys.

CASS. Yes . . . yes—one would have to come back. (*He moves up the stairs to the window and looks out.*) Has there been much—excavation on those megalithic stones ?

HERDA. One or two professors have been here to see them ; they do believe there is a buried village. Do you enjoy trout fishing, Mr. Cass ?

(CASS *turns down stage and puts his hands in his trouser pockets.*)

CASS. I used to—— (*He comes down the stairs.*)

HERDA. Now is a splendid time for it, and you could have no more amiable companion than my niece.

CASS (*coming down to the tea-table*). It's hard to believe she's your niece, you look more like sisters !

HERDA (*looking up*). How very complimentary of you ! But I am eight years older than Abby. (*She rises.*)

CASS. Then she cannot be more than twelve.

HERDA (*laughing*). Sometimes she's not a day more. (*She leaves her work in the chair and goes up to the conservatory window.*) It's going to be lovely weather for you. I am glad. (*She stands* L. *of the window.*)

(CASS *follows her up to* R., *of the window.*)

CASS (*staring across the bay*). White sand ! There aren't many places in England where the sand is white. (*He leans against the pillar between the windows. He takes his hands out of his pockets.*)

HERDA. The friend I was telling you about once likened it to Australia. There is a stretch of sand at a place called Portsea.

CASS. The sand there is white—like sugar—and hot to touch. (*His hands move as though sensitive to the heat and the feel of the grass.*) And a strange buffalo grass cuts into your flesh when you brush against it.

HERDA. But that's——

CASS (*turning to* HERDA). Are you sure your niece has never left the Islands ?

HERDA. Quite sure—why do you ask me that ?

CASS. I thought—no, I was sure, I had met her before——

HERDA. Perhaps you have been in the Orkneys ?

CASS. No. (*He pauses. He shakes his head slowly, smiling suddenly.*) It must only be in my dreams—there are a lot of places like that. I can feel them suddenly with my hands—they're familiar—friendly. Yes, that's it, friendly. (*He seems to be talking to himself.*)

HERDA. You've been here ? In a dream ? How—how strange——

CASS. I know the feel of that drunken little tree out there— (*he looks out at it*) sticky . . . and the lichen on the stones . . . I've sat on the Skerry and I know what I will see at the turn of the hill.

HERDA. Mr. Cass, I've never seen you before, but there *is* something—familiar—I thought it must be your poetry—one can know a person by his writings. (*She hesitates.*)

(CASS *waits for her to go on.*)

(*She smiles shyly.*) I—I read a great deal. I have loved all your poetry. No, that's not quite true.

(*They face one another across the window.*)

I didn't love your last one that came out in the " Blue Book," and——

CASS. You didn't ?

HERDA. No, I—I'm afraid I was a little shocked.

CASS. Shocked ?

HERDA. It was—it seemed so unlike the *you* I thought I knew. Forgive me, it seemed a tragedy that a man so full of promise, so excitingly full of promise, should—change so integrally.

CASS. I wrote nothing for nearly two years. I've been ill, you know—it's only lately I tried again——

HERDA (*contritely*). Oh, I know !—I'm so sorry—it—it was just another poet writing, a man of—of——

CASS (*eagerly*). A man of—what ?

HERDA (*smiling and shaking her head*).   There was no beauty in that last poem.

CASS.   It was not meant to be beautiful, Miss Herda.   (*He leans towards her.*)   It was meant to be bitter.   I know he meant it to be bitter—for he was a bitter man when he died——·

HERDA.   He ?——

(CASS *turns down stage and crosses to* C.   *He doesn't answer.*)

It was ugly, and knowing all the others and seeing you now I know it wasn't you who wrote it.   (*She turns down stage and stands in the middle of the window.*)

CASS (*standing with his back to* HERDA).   No—it wasn't I wrote it.   I can't write anything—nothing comes, nothing.   (*He turns up to her.*)   Forgive me.   Leaning my troubles on you the moment we meet.   (*He goes up to her.*)   I'm very sorry !   (*He stands* L. *of the window with his back to the audience.*)

HERDA.   Oh, I do hope . . . it would be so lovely if you could feel well enough to write while you are up here with us—regain yourself.

(CASS *looks off along the staircase.*)

CASS.   Would it ?   I wonder.   Perhaps I'm infused with something that is better—strength instead of frustrated beauty.

HERDA.   I do hope that you will want to write here. . . . (*She turns to the conservatory.*)   I know the Islands will want to help, and to a writer they should be a thrilling inspiration, because they are never the same for two hours at a time—and the wind !   Ah, forgive me for my presumption. . . . Ah, look, aren't they beautiful !   (*She moves out into the conservatory.*)

(CASS *follows her.*)

CASS (*looking up at the sky*).   What are they—Skua gulls ?

HERDA.   No, they're Weig's.

CASS.   Wigs ?

HERDA.   Kittiwakes.   And that smaller one sitting on the wall is called in Island words—Blue Maa !

CASS.   Aren't they wonderful ? . . . They seem to be shouting something at me !

HERDA.   Shouting at you ?

(CASS *turns down stage and looks up, listening.*)

CASS.   Yes . . . Can't you hear them ?   Guy—Guy—Guy——!   There it is—— (*He listens for a moment and then turns back up stage again.*)

HERDA (*nodding*).   This is the most wonderful place for birds if you're interested. . . . Look, that's the Tangie Maa, which is the smallest gull—and quite often we have a . . .

CASS (*interrupting and pointing*). Look, look ! What's that one down by the wall ?

HERDA. That's a Herra Gus—a goose of some kind, I forget his name. (*She turns down stage and comes into the room, to the back of the settee.*)

CASS (*turning and moving to the pillar between the windows*). I believe you get a wish if you see your first goose in flight !

HERDA (*turning to him*). Do you ? Oh—wish—wish.

(CASS *closes his eyes tightly, holding his gloved hands over them.* HERDA'S *face changes as she sees the gloves at closer quarters. He opens his eyes, looking at her through the fingers.*)

CASS. Can you tell fortunes ?

HERDA. Yes, how did you know ?

CASS. Because I'm a reader of faces ! (*He looks through his hands at her.*)

HERDA (*embarrassed*). Oh, forgive me ! I was just——

(ABIGAIL *enters down the stairs. She is smiling.*)

CASS (*turning to* ABIGAIL). Hullo ! (*He moves to the foot of the stairs.*) Your sister is going to tell my fortune !

HERDA. Isn't he absurd ! (*She turns to the fireplace.*) He will insist that I am your sister and that you are twelve years old. (*She stands with her back to the fireplace.*)

ABIGAIL. Am I ? (*She hesitates on the bottom stair.*)

CASS. There is something about you that is twelve.

ABIGAIL. That is because you knew me when I was twelve and I was happy, and some of it got left behind.

CASS. But where ? Where was it ? That's what we must find out.

(ABIGAIL *smiles without answering.*)

You *know* and you won't tell me !

(ABIGAIL *shakes her head slowly.*)

I know ! I was twelve too and I lived across the Bay and taught you how to fish and make a catapult !

(ABIGAIL'S *smile fades, her eyes widen slowly, a look of almost terror flashing across her face. She breaks from* CASS *and crosses below the settee to down stage of* HERDA.)

HERDA (*hurriedly*). Some people never seem to have been children—and some children never seem to grow any older. I think Abby is one of those !

ABIGAIL (*standing beside* HERDA ; *gaily*). What shall we do tomorrow ! You can choose anything.

(CASS *turns and moves to* C.)

HERDA.  I've been telling Mr. Cass——
ABIGAIL (*correcting her*).  Stephen——
CASS.  Thank you——
HERDA.  I've been telling Stephen what a good fisherman you are.
ABIGAIL (*gravely*).  He knows . . . but I've fished alone for years——

(SARCLET *enters down the stairs.*)

SARCLET.  I suppose no one thought to offer Stephen a whisky and soda ?  (*He goes to the serving-table.*)
HERDA.  Oh !
CASS.  Please !  I didn't want one anyway.
SARCLET (*pouring out a drink*).  And what have you all been talking about behind my back ?—Me ?
CASS.  No.
SARCLET.  Oh !
HERDA.  Isn't it strange, Edward, Stephen has a feeling he has been here before !  And his last poem might have been written about Skail !  Don't you agree ?
ABIGAIL.  *It is Skail.*

(SARCLET, *his drink in his hand, turns to* ABIGAIL, *hesitates, and is just about to speak when the gong goes.  He drinks.*)

HERDA.  There's dinner.  (*She crosses to* CASS.)  I ordered a meal early, I thought after your long journey you could do with some refreshment.  Shall we go in, Stephen ?

(HERDA *and* CASS *move towards the archway.*)

SARCLET (*as they pass him*).  Whisky, Stephen ?
CASS (*by the stairs*).  No, thank you.

(HERDA *and* CASS *exit through the archway.*  ABIGAIL *crosses to below the stairs.*)

SARCLET.  Abigail——

(ABIGAIL *turns.*  SARCLET *pours out another drink.*)

Don't be upset or worried if Stephen seems a little strange or says anything which may appear odd to you.  (*He moves down to* ABIGAIL.)
ABIGAIL.  No ?
SARCLET.  He suffered a tremendous shock when he had the accident—it—it makes him more imaginative than ever.
ABIGAIL.  Does it, Father ?
SARCLET.  Sometimes I wonder—if perhaps——

(ABIGAIL *watches him.*)

—the shock has been too great.
CURTAIN.

## SCENE 2

SCENE.—*The same. Three hours later.*

*The strange iridescent light of the Orkney sky contrasts sharply against the black outlined figure of* ABIGAIL, *leaning against the pillar between the windows, looking off* L. *Sitting on the settee at the* R. *end, with the lamplight falling across her hair,* HERDA *is unravelling silks for her embroidery. She looks up as the lamp on the piano flickers and nearly goes out, then she goes on with her unravelling.*

HERDA. Don't take cold——
ABIGAIL. Herda, have you seen him before ?
HERDA. No——

(*There is a long moment's silence between them again.*)

ABIGAIL. I do like him, Herda.
HERDA. Do you, my darling ?

(ABIGAIL *turns into the room.*)

ABIGAIL (*coming down between the settee and the chair* C.). What were you talking about when I came down ?
HERDA. Poetry. He seems unhappy about his poetry, which is sad. He seems restless and agitated. He's utterly charming and most amusing I found him at dinner . . .
ABIGAIL. I'm so *happy*, Herda, I've never been so happy—since . . . (*She crosses* HERDA *and sits on the fire-stool.*)
HERDA (*cutting in*). Is that why you gave him the Vendetta ?
ABIGAIL. That was strange—because I had given him that before I knew I wanted to ! . . . I hope he stays with us a long time. I hope I can wake up in the mornings and say to myself . . . he's here ! . . . he's here !

(HERDA *looks at her, smiling and happy.*)

HERDA. Poor fellow, he looks ill——
ABIGAIL. Did you notice his hands ? . . .
HERDA. Yes—I didn't realize, really, that something must be wrong with them . . . it was slow and stupid of me and then at dinner when he whispered with that funny little smile I could have died willingly !
ABIGAIL. What did he whisper ?
HERDA. He said, " You must forgive them, they are sown on."
ABIGAIL. He said that ?
HERDA. I was just about to ask him why he had sown his gloves on when——
ABIGAIL. No—but—that was not what he meant——

HERDA.   What else could he have meant ?

(ABIGAIL *rises and crosses to* C.)

What else ?

ABIGAIL.   Perhaps he meant that his hands were sown on——

HERDA (*laughing*).   Abby ! What a funny, terrible idea !
As if such a thing were possible !

(ABIGAIL *turns to her and the laugh dies as* HERDA *sees her face.*)

ABIGAIL.   We mustn't laugh.   Because that is the truth.

(HERDA *looks at her in astonishment.*)

HERDA.   But, darling, where did you get such an idea ?

ABIGAIL.   It is the truth, I tell you !

HERDA (*quietly*).   How do you know it is the truth ?

ABIGAIL.   Father told me.   He said I was not to tell you.

HERDA.   Because he thought I should not believe it ?

ABIGAIL.   He said that Stephen had suffered a dreadful
accident . . . and he lost his hands.

HERDA.   Oh ! . . .  But . . . he . . . has hands ! . . .

ABIGAIL.   Yes——

HERDA.   But—how ?

ABIGAIL.   They were taken off another man.   A dead man.

HERDA.   How . . . magnificent !

ABIGAIL.   Magnificent ?

HERDA.   If it's true, it's the most magnificent thing I've ever
heard !

ABIGAIL.   Oh, it's true all right.   Father was so mad with
excitement . . . (*she goes up to the window*) he's expecting it to
come out in that medical magazine of his—the " Lancet "—I
didn't think of it as—anything, but horrifying.   (*She comes down
to the chair* C.)

HERDA.   But it isn't horror—it's triumph——

ABIGAIL.   I hadn't reached the triumph—to me it was only
pain——

HERDA.   Edward is a surgeon of supreme excellence.   This
must be something quite new . . . something opening a door to
a world of new possibilities for the alleviation of pain. . . .   To
think that Stephen has *hands* where he might have had—nothing.
(*She stares out front.*)

ABIGAIL.   I didn't think of it that way.

HERDA.   But you must, hinnie.   The world is full of undis-
covered wonders.   Stephen and Edward have found something
and now lots of people will benefit.   I shouldn't be surprised if
Edward isn't one of the greatest living surgeons by the time he's
an old man.

ABIGAIL.   How strange you are, Herda.   You are far more
like Edward than I am.   I could only think about the—dead
man.

HERDA (*simply*). He was dead.

ABIGAIL. What must his family have thought ? . . . (*She moves to the foot of the stairs.*) Why did they choose that particular man ?

HERDA. Darling, we don't know all the circumstances . . .

ABIGAIL. It seemed as though he stood behind me, (*she moves down to the piano*) and I heard his voice say, " Pity me, pity me ! " Do you think he watches Stephen from where he is now ? Watches his hands, I mean ? Tries to talk to him——

HERDA. Darling, you are too imaginative . . . you should go to England for a while.

ABIGAIL (*taking a step towards* HERDA). I wanted to go away once . . . and you wouldn't let me, if you remember !

HERDA. Because that wasn't the time to go away. That was the time to stay near Herda and Fletty and people who loved you.

ABIGAIL. That was only two years ago . . . two days . . . two hours . . . dear ! How I ran that night ! The curve of the Bay had never seemed so long, and the stones cut into my feet, but I never felt anything, only a heavy lump on my chest— and the cold cold of the Northern Lights. (*She looks to the window.*)

HERDA. Let's not talk of it. It distresses me to remember your unhappiness.

(ABIGAIL *smiles.*)

Tomorrow is going to be lovely, you should take Stephen fishing if there's no fog.

ABIGAIL. If the fog hangs low over Harray, no matter what wind is blowing, no trout will rise. (*She crosses to the* L. *end of the settee.*) I believe he would find sea trout more amusing.

(CASS *and* SARCLET *enter through the archway* L. SARCLET *carries a whisky and soda.*)

CASS. More amusing than whom ?

(ABIGAIL *turns and smiles.*)

ABIGAIL (*moving above the* L. *end of the settee*). We were talking about trout fishing.

SARCLET (*crossing to the chair down* R.). Couldn't have a better fisherman than Abby. (*He sits.*)

CASS (*crossing above the chair* C. *to* ABIGAIL). What do you find best up here, March Brown and Red Heckle ?

ABIGAIL. Teal and Red is the best for now.

CASS. The Professor is one I like using.

ABIGAIL. If it's a bright day the Zulu is the best killing fly, Stephen, and if it's a dark day we ought to use the Cardinal.

HERDA. It won't be a dark day, it's going to be lovely.

SARCLET.   You'll have to be careful not to fall about, Cassius, or you might get an unlucky scratch !

CASS.   Don't worry !   I don't want another two years' hard labour !

ABIGAIL.   You'll be in good hands with me . . . oh ! . . .

(*She suddenly realizes the significance of her words and, in her confusion, looks at his hands.*)

SARCLET.   Smoke, Cass ?

CASS.   No, thanks.

SARCLET.   No slave to Lady Nicotine ?—Or do you use a clay pipe ?

ABIGAIL (*looking up at* CASS).   What would you use a clay pipe for ?

CASS.   Edward is asking if I blow bubbles !

ABIGAIL.   And do you ?

CASS (*looking at* SARCLET).   Yes.   But they burst—don't they ?

(ABIGAIL *moves up to the window and into the conservatory.* CASS *turns and watches her.   Then he comes below the settee to* HERDA.)

(*As he regards her work.*)   Is that going to be a football jersey, Miss Herda ?

HERDA.   No, it's a bag.   I'm not very good at it . . . I think I like doing the paintings on the terra-cotta plates better ; they require less concentration.

SARCLET.   What about some music ?   Abigail ?   Play for us and soothe our ragged nerves——

ABIGAIL.   I would rather not.

HERDA.   Yes, darling—and sing something.

ABIGAIL (*turning into the window*).   What about Stephen ?

CASS.   Oh, no.

SARCLET.   This is something new !   I seem to remember that ugly little upright at Vogespiegel being afforded little mercy.

CASS.   I don't play now.

ABIGAIL.   And I don't sing.   (*She comes into the room.*)

SARCLET.   Come, Cassius, we shall forgive your blunders.

HERDA.   Poor Stephen, you embarrass him, if he doesn't want to play.

SARCLET.   Cassius shall play—and Abigail shall sing.   Go on, Cassius, I insist.

CASS.   I dread it when Edward insists.   (*He crosses to the piano.*)   He shouldn't be allowed to have his own way so much.   (*He sits on the duet-stool.*)

(ABIGAIL *crosses to the piano.   She stands above the stool.*)

Especially in his own house.   (*He looks through the music on the piano top.*)  What shall we play ?  Here we are.  Sing this little Norwegian song.

ABIGAIL (*looking at the music over his shoulder*).  Why did you choose that one ?

CASS (*surprised*).  I happen to know it, it's one of my favourites . . . I think I can manage it.  (*He looks at the music.*)

ABIGAIL (*moving to* CASS'S R. *elbow*).  Oh, I haven't sung that one for years . . . it always makes me cry.

SARCLET.  Sing it.  I'm in the mood for anything.

(CASS *starts playing the introduction.*)

(*To* HERDA.)  I am glad it's not going to be " Annie Laurie " !

HERDA.  Or " Stay Steersman."

(CASS *finishes the introduction and starts the song.  HERDA looks up at* ABIGAIL.  ABIGAIL *starts singing in a clear round childish voice that is a delight.  CASS looks up at her and smiles.  At the end of the song* SARCLET *looks at* HERDA.  *She nods.*)

SARCLET.  Bravo !

CASS (*quietly*).  That was most lovely.

ABIGAIL.  It's a sad little song.

CASS.  Who taught you to sing that so beautifully ?

(ABIGAIL *turns up stage and moves to the foot of the stairs.*)

ABIGAIL (*her jaw setting*).  Nobody taught me anything at all. I learned myself to everything I know.  (*She goes up four stairs.*)

(HERDA *smiles.*  SARCLET'S *eyebrows go up.*)

CASS.  Thank you for singing it.  (*He plays the song again, loudly.*)

(ABIGAIL *moves up on to the half-landing.  CASS continues the song more softly to himself.*)

SARCLET (*breaking in on the music*).  How do they feel, Cassius ?

CASS.  All right.  Not much pressure.  I'm a little out of practise.

(ABIGAIL *looks out of the window.*)

SARCLET.  Sounds as good as ever.  Better.

CASS.  It is better, isn't it, Edward ?  (*He turns to* SARCLET *and stops playing.*)  Much better than when I played on that funny little square upright at Vogespiegel !  I thought *that* when I played on the hospital piano—he liked playing that piano, I think——

(SARCLET *realizes what* CASS *has said.  He rises and crosses to the serving-table.*)

SARCLET (*firmly*).   You always played well.

(CASS *turns on the stool and faces* SARCLET.)

CASS.   But, Edward—would that be from habit or from my brain—from me—would——

SARCLET.   You, of course !   You !—Herda and Abigail must find our conversation dull and rude.

(HERDA *looks up.*)

CASS (*turning to* ABIGAIL *and* HERDA).   Forgive me—you must wonder what on earth——

SARCLET.   Cassius !   The time is not ripe.   Don't say too much.

ABIGAIL (*on the stairs ; turning to* SARCLET).   Why is it not ?   We all know you are talking about Stephen's hands——

SARCLET (*with a look at her*).   It's a long story and we are tired after our journey.

(HERDA *rises and crosses down to the chair down* R., *below the fire.*)

CASS.   I'm not tired, Edward.   If they would like me to tell them——

HERDA.   Please, Stephen.   (*She sits.*)

(SARCLET *moves to the window.*)

CASS.   Do you mind, Edward ?   After all, you expect the " Lancet " here any day and for my part, I should be happier—I should like them to know——

SARCLET.   No, I don't mind . . . if it's not tonight it will be tomorrow——   (*He moves down to the chair* C. *and sits.*)

(CASS *stares for a moment at* SARCLET'S *back.*)

CASS.   This is a very wonderful story.

(HERDA *and* ABIGAIL *watch* CASS *in silence.*)

Two years ago I was climbing a mountain . . . the—the rope got twisted in some rocks . . . a boulder got shifted and rolled down . . . my hands were jellied !

(HERDA *and* ABIGAIL *never take their eyes off him ; he laughs nervously, holding his hands tight.*)

After a lot of " pully-hawly " I was taken back to England, clinging to the jellies, of course—or rather, they were still clinging to me—hanging by a thread, literally ! . . . Edward—(*he pauses*)—he tried to do something with them—but they weren't hands any more ! . . . He took them off. (*Gravely.*) The miracle about that operation was that I wasn't presented with two hooks as I suspected—I was kept under even longer than nature already had planned for me . . . and when I opened my eyes upon a strange world of pain . . . I had . . . hands . . . (*Quietly.*) That's all. (*He smiles suddenly, a brilliant, devastating smile ; the smile of a man who could sob.*)

(HERDA *looks down quickly at her silks.*)

HERDA. That was—wonderful. (*To* SARCLET.) Edward you are indeed a truly great surgeon. How pleased and proud our father would have been had he heard Stephen speak—and the medical profession ! Now they must admit it at last !

SARCLET. " They called me misbeliever, cut-throat, dog ! "

CASS (*leaning forward*). Tell them, Edward, tell your sister what you did——

HERDA. Tell us, Edward. It is such a tremendous achievement.

(ABIGAIL *never takes her eyes off* CASS'S *face. There is a little smile about her lips.*)

SARCLET (*sitting forward and embracing them all*). No one would believe such an operation possible ! I sutured the blood vessels and tendons . . . I watched the nerve ends growing correctly—half an inch a month . . . the muscles exercised by a co-operative patient . . . that's all . . . and there he is with two perfect hands . . . carpals, metacarpals, and phalanges— where he had pulp ! There is nothing more to it. (*He rises and turns towards* CASS *as he goes up to the serving-table.*) Nature did the rest—he is as well as he ever was (*with a smile at* CASS) save that his brain is a little touched. (*He pours out a drink.*)

CASS. You misunderstand, Edward. It is my heart that is touched.

HERDA. There's just one thing I should like to ask you, Edward, may I ?

(SARCLET *frowns.*)

SARCLET. What is it ? (*He looks at* CASS.)

HERDA. The hands . . . you don't mind me saying this, Stephen ?

CASS. No. (*He faces* HERDA.)

HERDA. The hands . . . where . . . whose were they ?

SARCLET. They came from a man—a dead man. (*He drinks.*)

(ABIGAIL'S *forehead is knitted.*)

ABIGAIL (*turning to the stair-rail and looking down on* SARCLET). Why that man—why those hands ?

(*There is an imperceptible pause.*)

SARCLET. Because it happened to *be* that man ! It might have been another. He gave them to me. He sent for me—to take them. He wished me to take them.

ABIGAIL. What do you mean ?

CASS. In the same way that people bestow their bodies to the Royal College of Surgeons . . . he bestowed his hands—he knew about me, he knew he was going to die—he gave his hands to Edward for me—I owe him—life——

HERDA. How heroic.

CASS. —and something more——

HERDA. To be able to think so selflessly !

SARCLET (*coming down* c.). He sent for me. (*He turns and faces up stage.*) He believed I could do it—if he hadn't believed so strongly I might not have done it.

ABIGAIL (*coming down the stairs*). Why should he want to help Stephen—did he know him ?

SARCLET (*moving towards the settee*). Every one knew him—people were much distressed.

HERDA. He must have died happy, knowing——

ABIGAIL (*at the foot of the stairs ; looking at* CASS). Does he—does he make himself known to you in any way, Stephen ?—Because such a man couldn't die——

CASS. I know him, yes, indeed ! I know quite a lot about him—he isn't dead to me.

(SARCLET *turns his eyes on him.*)

ABIGAIL. Perhaps he had some reason for wanting his hands to go on—some work unfinished, perhaps he hoped that you——

CASS. You think that too ! . . . I *know* it—everywhere I go . . .

SARCLET (*breaking in*). Nonsense ! There was no question of anything like that ! He was just endeavouring to assist human nature to better surgery . . .

HERDA. Did *you* know him, Edward ? Had you known him before ?

SARCLET. No . . . (*He sits on the settee.*)

ABIGAIL. But you must have seen him ! Where was he ?

(CASS *watches* SARCLET *eagerly.*)

SARCLET (*snorting*). I saw him, of course ! How else—he was —as good as dead when I saw him. I wish people didn't have to ask so many futile questions ! " What did he look like ?—Was he young ?—Good-looking ?—Tall or short, fat or thin, man or devil ? " I tell you I'm disgusted by the morbidity of you ladies ! He was *just a man*—let him rest in peace !

ABIGAIL (*moving to above the chair* c.). P'raps he doesn't want to—p'raps he didn't want to die either—p'raps he fretted—— (*She turns to* CASS.)

CASS. Fretted ? (*He turns his eyes on her.*)

SARCLET. Let us change the topic.

HERDA. Why did he die ? What was wrong that he should die ?

(SARCLET *waves his hand angrily.*)

SARCLET. He had to die! He died—of—dilation of the heart. . . . He . . . they tell me he was a man of infinite humour. . . . Play something, Cassius. I'm tired of this talk——

ABIGAIL. Father is afraid we might bring back his spirit——

SARCLET (*rising*). Now no more of it! Be silent!

HERDA. I should like to know more of this man.

SARCLET. It never occurs to you that it might distress Stephen.

HERDA. Oh!

SARCLET (*moving round the* R. *end of the settee to the back of it*). You put ideas and distress into his mind.

CASS. No—I like to talk of him. I think of him a great deal.

SARCLET. I'm going out, then you can talk as you like. (*He goes up to the window.*)

CASS (*rising*). I'll come too! (*He goes up* C.)

SARCLET (*turning*). You've had enough for one day. Go to bed. Herda, see he goes to bed early.

(*He goes out through the conservatory.* CASS *looks disappointed. He turns* R. *and returns to the piano-stool.*)

CASS (*sitting*). I hope I didn't do wrong in making Edward talk about it. He was wonderful . . . watching, and encouraging when I would have thrown the wretched things out of the window! (*He fingers a few notes.*)

ABIGAIL. Yes, play something. I don't want to talk about it either. (*She sits in the chair* C.)

CASS. I'm sorry——

HERDA. Abby, that's a little rough way to speak.

(CASS *starts to play the Norwegian Love Song.*)

CASS. Let's sing your song again . . . I quite fell in love with you singing that. (*He looks down smiling, reluctant to say too much.*)

ABIGAIL. No, I won't sing any more . . . You play . . .

(CASS *leaves off the Love Song and starts fingering the notes.*)

CASS. There was a piano in the hospital, and I used to try and play it to get my hands exercised. I used to try and make things up . . . but I only really succeeded with one—listen and tell me if you like it.

(ABIGAIL *looks at* HERDA. *Then she rises and moves over to the piano.* CASS *starts to play the Boat Song, quietly and simply. His body sways slightly to the beat. The smile fades from* ABIGAIL'S *face.* HERDA *looks up astonished. Then a great joy breaks across* ABIGAIL'S *face.*)

ABIGAIL. Stephen! Oh, Stephen, where did you hear that? How strange that you should play it.

CASS (*smiling as he plays*). You like it, eh?

ABIGAIL. Like it! But of course I like it! I love it! Tell me, tell me where you heard it! Who played it for you?

CASS (*without looking up*). It's mine! I made it up!

ABIGAIL. Yours! No, no, Stephen, don't tease me! . . .

(CASS *stops playing.*)

Where, oh *where* was it played to you?

(*Only then does* CASS *look up.*)

CASS (*turning to* ABIGAIL). I've told you the truth, Abigail, I'm not teasing—I made it up. It's mine . . . I've never heard anyone play it in my life . . . I made it up at the hospital.

ABIGAIL. But—that's not possible! You, you can't have made it up, Stephen! You can't! You must have heard it! I—*I've* heard it—often—played by someone quite different, haven't I, Herda?

HERDA. Many times, Stephen, here in this room—on that piano. (*She rises.*)

CASS. You've heard it before? You know it?—what is it called—what music is it then?

ABIGAIL (*looking at* HERDA *and speaking quickly*). It's a Chinese Boat Song . . . it came from the Min River—when the tea boats come in at sunset they sing it. . . . (*She turns to* CASS.) I expect you heard Father play it. Or—or someone a long time ago? Yes, that was it, wasn't it? At a party perhaps, or coming from an open window—— (*She drops on her knees beside him.*) Think! think!

(CASS *shakes his head, turns to the keyboard and starts to play it again as if to convince himself.*)

CASS (*after a few bars*). No, no, I'm sure!—*sure!*—It was in the hospital I found it—no one ever played there but me . . . it didn't come at first . . . it wasn't easy . . . I worked on it . . . A Boat Song, you say? . . . No, I wish I could help you . . . I wish I could . . . but no, *no*! I never heard anyone play it. (*He looks at* ABIGAIL.) Who played it on this piano? Edward?

(SARCLET *enters through the conservatory and stands in the window. They do not see him.*)

HERDA. Abigail dear——

(CASS *strikes the chords, playing it well, and wonderfully, with all its nostalgia and yearning.*)

CASS. Who played this music to you, Abigail? Who was it?

ABIGAIL (*looking at* HERDA). It was—it was . . .

(SARCLET *smashes his hand against the window.* ABIGAIL *is bewildered, her face crumples.* SARCLET *stands there, eyes blazing.* CASS *stops playing abruptly, his hands poised over the keys. His eyes turn and meet* SARCLET'S, *which are glassy. With a sudden sob,* ABIGAIL *rises and hurries towards the stairs.* HERDA *crosses and follows her off quickly. She goes up them and off* L.)

CASS. What is it, Edward ? What are you looking so angry about ?

(SARCLET *stands watching him, a thousand thoughts fleeing through his dark eyes, then without a word he walks across the room and up the stairs.*)

Edward !

(SARCLET *stops on the half-landing and looks off* L.)

Where *is* this person who plays my music ?

(SARCLET *answers him not, but goes up the rest of the stairs and exits.* CASS *continues to sit, bewildered. He looks at his hands, then turns to the piano and starts to play the Boat Song. After four bars the piano off stage takes up the melody.* CASS *stops, turns and listens. The offstage piano plays four bars and then stops.* CASS *turns to the piano and plays again ; the offstage piano takes up the counter-melody.* CASS *stops and the offstage piano continues eight bars.* CASS *turns and looks at his hands, and then up to the ceiling. When the offstage piano stops he turns and plays to the end of the song, the offstage piano taking up the melody with him. When he stops at the end of the song the offstage piano plays the echo of the last three chords.* CASS *turns to* C.)

(*Looking at his hands.*) What is it ? What *is* it you want me to do ?

SLOW CURTAIN.

# ACT II

## Scene 1

Scene.—*The same. The following morning.*

*Brilliant sun pours through the open windows on to the saxe-blue carpet, and the air is heavy with the scent of roses and the cries of the kittiwakes as they wheel in from the dazzling sand of the Bay.*

Abigail *is doing the roses. When the* Curtain *rises she is up by the serving-table pouring water into the bowl on it from a small watering-can. This done she goes into the conservatory with the can and off* L. *She returns immediately with another bowl of roses, crosses up* R. *with them and puts them on the revolving bookcase.*

Herda *enters through the archway* L. *She has a pile of linen in her arms and moves to the stairs.*

Abigail. He hasn't run away, has he ?

Herda (*laughing*). Gracious, no !

Abigail. He isn't in his room. He had a cup of tea terribly early, Fletty says—in the kitchen !

Herda. He's gone for a walk, I dare say——

(Herda *starts up the* L. *side of the stairs.* Abigail *runs to the bottom of the stairs, by the* R. *balustrade.*)

Abigail (*in a low voice*). Herda !

(Herda *pauses on the half-landing and turns down to her.*)

Herda. Yes ?

Abigail. Don't let him go away——

(Herda *looks down into the beautiful eyes with great affection.*)

Herda. Abby !——

Abigail. I just know that I couldn't bear it if he left . . . I know I don't mean anything to him at all—how could I . . . but perhaps—(*she turns away towards the serving-table*)—if he stayed a little while longer——

Herda. Abby !——

Abigail. I was awake all night . . . something . . . he's . . . I don't know what it is, Herdy. . . . (*She turns suddenly to* Herda *and runs up the stairs to her.*) Oh, Herda !

(*She throws herself at* Herda *and knocks the linen all down the stairs.* Herda's *face over her shoulder is a little troubled.*)

HERDA.  Go easy, my hinnie . . . don't let yourself get hurt again. . . .

(ABIGAIL *looks up quickly*.)

ABIGAIL.  You mean you think he'll never . . .

HERDA.  No, no, I don't mean that . . . but—please, darling, don't show it !—Hug it to your secret heart . . . keep it hidden lest you . . . don't pursue it too closely—let it grow . . . let it grow . . . you can't force big issues—like birth and death, except by violence . . . tread lightly, my hinnie——

(ABIGAIL *breaks away*.)

ABIGAIL.  You don't think it can ever be ?  You speak as though you had a fear . . .

HERDA.  I have a fear, Abby—deep in my heart I have a fear . . . but I'm sure it's the fear for you . . . the fear of you being hurt again . . .

ABIGAIL (*crossing to the* R. *balustrade*).  Oh, Herda !  If you knew how I feel !  How my heart is jumping and singing . . . how suddenly, all pain of other things has left me . . . I feel released !  Free ! . . .  (*She turns to* HERDA.)  Oh, Herda, is it wrong to be too happy ?  Or can I put it against those other years ?

HERDA.  Some people believe you have to pay in kind for happiness . . .

ABIGAIL (*going to* HERDA).  And you ?  What do you believe ?

HERDA.  I don't know . . . I only know you have to hang on to things while you have them . . .

(ABIGAIL *doesn't answer, and they stand there together, the shaft of light from the leaded window striking across Abigail's brilliant hair.* CASS *walks in through the conservatory and the window* C. *He has on a white shirt and flannel trousers, and carries a towel slung over his shoulder.* HERDA *sees him and gently puts* ABIGAIL *from her.* ABIGAIL *immediately drops down on her knees and starts to pick up the linen on the landing.*)

Good morning !  Sleep well ?

CASS.  Very well, thank you.  (*He sees the linen down the stairs.*)  Hullo, what's happened here ?

HERDA.  Abigail and I had an accident with the linen !

(CASS *comes to the foot of the stairs by the* R. *balustrade and sees* ABIGAIL, *who is over-busy collecting.*)

CASS.  Hullo !

ABIGAIL.  Good morning !

CASS.  Good morning !

ABIGAIL (*lightly*).  Been swimming ?

CASS. Yes. Very cold.

ABIGAIL. I know. But when I went in it was colder.

CASS. How was that ?

ABIGAIL. It was earlier !

CASS. You've been in earlier ! Why didn't you take me with you ?

ABIGAIL. Oh !—Well—you see, I don't wear anything.

HERDA. Abby !

(*She takes the linen from* ABIGAIL *and goes up the stairs and off.* CASS *crosses up* R. *above the settee to the revolving bookcase.* ABIGAIL *comes down to the piano and arranges the roses on it.*)

CASS (*picking up a packet*). Thank God ! The " Lancet ! " (*He comes down to the fireplace with it.*)

ABIGAIL. Why ?

CASS (*turning to her*). Why ? First public appearance of the operation ; Edward will be glad. I must take it to him. (*He crosses to the stairs.*)

ABIGAIL (*moving up to the foot of the stairs,* L. *side*). The Medical Board always treat him as if he were some kind of charlatan and——

(CASS *mounts one step.*)

CASS (*turning to her and interrupting*). Were you *never* in Vogespiegel ?

ABIGAIL. Did you never climb the Man of Hoy ?

CASS. Never.

ABIGAIL. Never—(*she crosses him and goes to the serving-table*) —I must away and do my flowers. It takes me all the morning and——

CASS (*turning to her, over the balustrade*). Why did you run upstairs last night, crying——?

ABIGAIL (*hotly*). I did not.

CASS. Oh, yes, you did. I heard you. It was because of the music, wasn't it ?—The Boat Song——?

ABIGAIL. It was nothing—I was sad suddenly, and when I'm sad tears come—it is nothing, it might happen any moment—it might happen now.

CASS. Who was it that played it to you ?

ABIGAIL. We don't say his name any more in this house. (*She turns away and faces down* R.)

CASS (*fiercely*). Why not ?—you must——!

ABIGAIL. He was a friend of Father's . . . he went away . . . Father forbade his name to be mentioned. (*She turns up stage and goes into the conservatory.*)

(ABIGAIL *goes off* L. *through the conservatory.* CASS *puts his towel on the balustrade, comes down the stairs and moves to the* L. *side of the window.* ABIGAIL *enters through the window and walks past him. She comes down between the settee and the chair* O. CASS *pauses a moment before speaking.*)

CASS. Were you in love with him ?

ABIGAIL (*stopping below the settee*). You have no right to ask questions.

CASS. Are you still ?

ABIGAIL. No—no——

CASS. Tell me his name. Perhaps I can find him for you, perhaps——

ABIGAIL. No——

(CASS *moves down to* ABIGAIL *to her* R.)

CASS. I need to find him ! He might be able to help me too——

ABIGAIL. No ! No !—you can never find him . . . (*She pauses.*) I wouldn't want you to if you could.

CASS. I must find him.

(*There is a pause.* ABIGAIL *crosses in front of him. As she passes* CASS *suddenly seizes her hand ; she cries out with the force of it, and something else she cannot understand. She stands with her back to him as she peels his fingers off her hand.*)

I'm sorry . . . Did I hurt you ? I wouldn't hurt you—I couldn't bear that—in case you cried again——

(ABIGAIL *shakes her head. He stands watching her, then she moves to the mantelpiece and once again she takes a scarlet bloom out of the Chelsea vase.*)

ABIGAIL. Stephen—— (*She turns and holds the rose out to him.*)

CASS. No !

(*But she continues to hold it out and he drops the "Lancet" on the tea-table and takes the rose.*)

ABIGAIL. Every day, as long as there are any blooms left, I shall give you one, and you must wear it !

CASS. Why do you say that ?

ABIGAIL. I don't know. (*She laughs and puts the rose in his buttonhole.*)

CASS (*smiling*). Is there some hidden meaning ?—Vendetta ! Am I to be revenged on because of some other ? That other who plays my music, perhaps ?

(ABIGAIL'S *smile fades.*)

ABIGAIL. No . . . no . . .

CASS. Have you sworn to plunge its thorns in all our hearts because of him ?—Have you, Abigail ?——

(*They stand looking at each other in silence.*)

ABIGAIL.  Oh, Stephen——

CASS (*almost in a whisper*).  Oh, Abigail . . . you rend my heart with your tears and your roses, and your folded hands.

(HERDA'S *and* SARCLET'S *voices are heard from the floor above.* ABIGAIL *stands watching the stairs, then turning suddenly, she runs off through the conservatory.* HERDA *enters down the stairs and just behind her* SARCLET.)

SARCLET.  These stairs have been like the scenic railway this morning !  Good morning, Cassius !

CASS.  Did you sleep badly, Edward ?

(HERDA *moves to the archway* L.)

SARCLET.  Exceedingly.  (*He pauses on the half-landing.*)

CASS.  Was that guilty conscience or just whisky ?

SARCLET.  It was neither, my dear fellow.  I suffer from none of these things.  It was the birds.  God, how I hate birds.  (*He looks out of the landing window.  To* HERDA.)  I've been thinking that I'll take Cassius over to Longhope—we might stay there with John for a week or so and get some fishing.  (*He comes to the bottom of the stairs.*)

CASS.  Is he the player of my music ?

(SARCLET *frowns.*)

HERDA (*surprised*).  But, Edward !  Stephen has hardly been here a minute !  And besides, Abby is a far more amusing companion than John Tweed.

SARCLET.  More amusing for whom ?

HERDA.  Well, Stephen, I suppose.

SARCLET.  We can come back—later.

HERDA.  Oh ! how disappointed Abby will be ;  and I, of course, too.

(CASS *takes the* " Lancet " *off the table and holds it up.*)

CASS.  Thank you, Miss Herda !  I see I am forgiven for my bad poetry.

SARCLET (*suddenly seeing what* CASS *is holding*).  The "Lancet !"  (*He crosses to* CASS *and takes it.*)

(CASS *breaks to the fireplace.*)

(*To* HERDA.)  Why didn't you tell me it had come !  (*He tears it open and moves to the settee.*)  I have been waiting for this.  (*He sits.*)

HERDA.  Well, I haven't had much chance !

(*There is a pause while* SARCLET *reads.*)

SARCLET.  Listen to this !  Glory at last !  At long last !

HERDA. I'm so glad for you, Edward. You do deserve pæans of praise. (*She crosses to the back of the chair* C.)

SARCLET. Listen to this, Cassius! "The word genius has been much bandied about in our generation, but in the person of Mr. Edward Sarclet, the eminent surgeon, never!"

HERDA. There!

CASS. There!

SARCLET. And this! "Mr. Edward Sarclet, the Orkney Wizard, holds the destiny of millions in the palm of his brilliant hand, let us hope he will not——" Oh well, needn't read all that . . .

(*He rises and advances on* HERDA. *She backs to the foot of the stairs.*)

It's come, Herda! Success, like a slow tide creeping towards me. Success! . . . Father had a spark, you know!—He passed it to me. I have more than a spark—I have a flame! (*He turns down stage to* CASS.)

HERDA. If only Francie had lived and given you a son.

(CASS *sits on the head of the bear-skin rug.*)

SARCLET (*turning back to* HERDA). Then he would probably have been as highly strung and idiotic as Francie . . . No, no—— (*He suddenly seizes her hand.*) Herda! I've just thought! You know what we'll do?

HERDA (*smiling, delighted at his confidence*). No? What? What will we do, Edward?

SARCLET. We'll have Whipcoll to celebrate!

(HERDA'S *smile fades.*)

HERDA. Whipcoll, Edward!—Do you think we ought to? Last time everyone got a little tipsy and if you remember it was a very unfortunate day!

SARCLET (*turning to* C.). Today is the day to get tipsy! Very, very tipsy.

HERDA. Edward—remember——

SARCLET. Remember what?

HERDA. It—I believe it is very strong drink made the way Fletty makes it——

SARCLET. Nonsense!—Nothing but malted milk and rum!—This is my day and I insist. Go on! Go and make it. Go and make it! (*He crosses to* HERDA *and pushes her towards the archway* L.)

(HERDA *hesitates a moment.* SARCLET *throws himself into the chair* C., *opens "The Lancet" again and reads with evident enjoyment. With a look at* CASS, HERDA *walks out* L.)

CASS. Does it give me a good review?—Am I in it?—Can I see it, Edward?

(SARCLET *passes the " Lancet " to* CASS.)

SARCLET. It's full of ripping statements about us both !

(CASS *reads. He raises his brows now and again, smiles and whistles.*)

(*After a moment*). Good, isn't it ?

CASS. Did you write it ? They've certainly said everything —if that's what you wanted.

SARCLET. Of course it's what I wanted, fathead !—I've been working for twenty years for a moment like this. . . . Want it !—I certainly want it, it'll make those octogenarians at the clubs sit up . . . that's what I wanted too.

CASS. Edward . . . you are an amazing man. (*He rises.*)

SARCLET. That's what the " Lancet " says !

CASS. But the " Lancet " doesn't know the amazing man that I know——  (*He moves to the settee and sits at the* R. *end.*)

SARCLET. Tell me. I love people talking about me.

CASS. You know what you've done and what you still can and will do, and yet until you see it all written down in print you almost doubt yourself ! Even over these—(*he holds out his hands*)—for a moment you doubted.

(SARCLET'S *eyebrows jerk forward.*)

SARCLET. How did you know !

CASS. You said so yourself, last night ; you've said so before too. You stand up to the world with one fist raised in anger and the other over your eyes. You threaten and you sneer and you destroy, yet if someone touches you on the shoulder you sob——

(SARCLET *laughs shortly.*)

SARCLET. I'm full of everything, Cassius. I'm as nervous as an hysterical woman !—I'm a mass of complexities and disorders, a tangled skein of jealousies and loves and promiscuous indiscriminate sex !—I'm my own worst enemy, trying to hide my diminished head because of my personal feeling of inferiority ! —God knows why I'm burdening you with this thesis on a fat man—but—well, I'm fond of you, Cassius, fonder of you than anyone, I suppose because I know you better—I wish I was a bit more like you—I wish someone would say of me that I was the " sworn companion of the wind "—I wish I could live like you—with zest—and die with—undiminished glory—like you will—I wish I had no Fear like you—but then you have no reason for fear—and I—stalk behind its shadow——

CASS. Why should you ? What should you have to fear ?

SARCLET (*rising*). I hate life and I fear death and everybody else hates me ! (*He crosses to the fireplace.*)

CASS (*breaking in*). Edward !

(SARCLET *takes down a miniature off a hook and then puts it back again.*)

SARCLET. I suppose I'm tired—I suddenly feel as if a good blub would be my salvation! (*He turns and sees* CASS's *face.*) No, no, don't worry! I won't do it! This holiday will do us both good—only—stay by me—I need you as much now as I needed you at Vogespiegel two years ago—I'm so damned lonely.

CASS. Do you realize, Edward, you've worked for two years on me, with little else but jeers from the crowd and curses from me . . . I can understand—it's replacement you need, rehabilitation. But for the rest you're wrong—you're a very individual person, Edward, a veritable Triton among minnows.

SARCLET (*turning his yellow eyes on* CASS; *gravely*). Thank you, Cassius . . . you have restored my crumbling equilibrium and staved off the humiliating dismals!

CASS (*laughing*). The real trouble with you is that you're bilious! (*He rises and turns to* SARCLET.) You drink too much whisky.

SARCLET. I have whisky in my veins instead of blood. Didn't you know?

CASS. Ah—that accounts for the ghastly sensational whites of your eyes! Can you see anything this morning?

SARCLET. How would you like a week at Longhope?

CASS. What's Longhope?

SARCLET. One of the Islands . . . John Tweed, a friend of mine across there, he has some wonderful guns and boats, and——

CASS. What's the matter with this place?

SARCLET. Girls. John Tweed is an excellent——

CASS. I like girls! I like these girls.

SARCLET. You'd have more fun there——

CASS. Fun?

SARCLET. No hysteria, except from me!—No vapours and embarrassments—only me——

CASS. No, no! I don't want to. (*He crosses to the foot of the stairs.*) I like this place and I'm getting along very nicely . . . your sister is charming and sweet, and—your daughter——

SARCLET. As alluring as a cat in love—— (*He moves to the settee.*) I think you're a fool not to come. (*He sits.*)

CASS. I think I'd be a fool to go! You don't want to go, do you? (*He moves down to the piano and sits on the stool.*)

SARCLET. I do want to go, but naturally if you won't——

CASS. No. I won't. (*He turns to* SARCLET *and looks at him. Then he turns back to the piano and strums on it.*)

SARCLET. Oh. How are they today?

CASS. All right.

(SARCLET *rises.* CASS *holds out his hands.* SARCLET *crosses to him and holds them, looking down at them closely.*)

SARCLET.  Don't go racketing about and messing the whole thing up.

CASS.  Wish you'd let the air get to the white-livered things.

SARCLET.  You said yourself——

CASS.  I know.  That was yesterday.  Today it's hot, and there's something positively perverted about swimming in white kid gloves !

(SARCLET *laughs and is about to reply when* ABIGAIL *enters through the conservatory.  She carries a basket.*)

ABIGAIL (*holding out the basket to* SARCLET).  Wild strawberries !  (*She comes down* L.C.).

SARCLET (*turning to her*).  Splendid !  And Herda Is making us Whipcoll !

(CASS *rises.*)

ABIGAIL (*surprised*).  Whipcoll !  You said—Whipcoll ?

SARCLET.  I said Whipcoll—Whipcoll—Whipcoll !  (*He breaks down* L. *and leans against the piano.*)

CASS.  What is Whipcoll ?

SARCLET.  Malted milk and rum !

ABIGAIL.  It's more than that, Stephen.  It's a Viking's drink . . . it . . . it's very strong . . . there's . . . it's what Brynhilde gave to Sigurd in a golden cup when he woke her from her magic sleep . . . they do say " drink Whipcoll and tell all your secrets ."

(CASS *smiles.*)

SARCLET.  It's heady stuff !—Not too much of it now, Abby !

(HERDA *enters through the archway* L. *with the bowl of Whipcoll.* FLETTY *follows her with a tray of glasses.*)

I hope it's good and strong for the Vikings, Herda !

HERDA (*quietly*).  It's the same as before.  (*She crosses to the serving-table and puts the bowl at the upstage end.*)

SARCLET.  Look at that poor field-mouse staggering under the weight of crystal.

(FLETTY *puts the tray of glasses on the serving-table.*)

FLETTY.  Ther's many a worse animal than a field-mouse— ther's a rat or a fox.

SARCLET.  The fox will bite off your head in a moment !

(HERDA *fills the glasses.  They stand around watching.*)

FLETTY (*with a look at* SARCLET).  This is verra strong drink, Mr. Cass.

(ABIGAIL *goes up to the serving-table.*)

CASS. Good.

FLETTY (*coming down* L. *with a glass*).   Tak the gypsy's warning—(*she gives the glass to* SARCLET) the last time we served it up——

SARCLET.   Give the miserable creature a glass, Herda, that's what she's angling for.

FLETTY (*returning to the serving-table*).   Enough is as gude as a feast.   You mind that, Edward.

SARCLET.   Oh, hush!

FLETTY.   One man's meat is anidder's poison——   (*She holds up her glass.*)   Da back a ma haand to da——   (*She lowers it.*)

SARCLET.   The back of my hand to you—you auld fule!——

(FLETTY *tosses it back and then exits through the archway* L. ABIGAIL *brings two glasses down and gives one to* CASS.  *For a split second their eyes hold.*)

ABIGAIL.   This is a golden cup.   (*She sits on the piano-stool.*)

CASS (*in a low voice*).   That sleep was too profound, Brynhilde . . .   (*He sits beside* ABIGAIL *on the piano-stool.*)

(SARCLET *looks up, suddenly aware . . . then he frowns and bangs hard on the piano with his fist.*)

SARCLET.   I give you a toast!

(*They all look at* SARCLET *expectantly.*)

Myself!

CASS.   Myself!

ABIGAIL.   Myself!

(ABIGAIL *and* CASS *drink deeply, their eyes laughing over the rims of their glasses.* HERDA *watches them and moves into the conservatory and off* R.)

SARCLET.   Abigail! that isn't the way to drink strong drink.

CASS.   Sometimes it is the only way!

(ABIGAIL *laughs.*)

SARCLET.   A fine way to behave.   (*He crosses to the serving-table and refills his glass.*)   I feel hurt and angry.   No congratulations, no pleasure in your father's success late in life!—Just sniggering with the patient.

ABIGAIL (*turning to him*).   Father!—Congratulations—Father——

(SARCLET *comes down* C. *with the bowl.   He puts it on the tea-table and sits in the chair* C.  CASS *rises and moves to* L. *of the chair* C.)

CASS (*raising his glass*).   Congratulations! . . . and—thank you, Edward.   (*He puts a hand on* SARCLET'S *shoulder.*)

SARCLET. Thanks! Now let us all sit down and become happily intoxicated.

(HERDA *enters through the conservatory.*)

HERDA (*coming down to the settee*). Edward! Supposing someone were to walk in! (*She sits.*)

SARCLET. Who would be so foolish? This is not a house of visitors.

(ABIGAIL *drinks deeply.*)

ABIGAIL. It was once. There was a time when—— (*She rises and crosses below* CASS *and* SARCLET *to the tea-table. As she passes* CASS *she takes his empty glass. She refills it and her own.*)

(CASS *moves up to the stairs and sits by the* L. *balustrade.*)

HERDA (*interrupting; quickly*). Dr. Macgowan might call on his way to Yesnaby.

SARCLET (*laughing*). Dr. Macgowan has never forgiven me for swinging on his beard at my christening.

CASS. He must be incredibly old.

(ABIGAIL *moves up to* CASS *and gives him his glass.*)

SARCLET. He is. (*He pauses.*) Drink up! Drink up! I wish to see you like Philistines lying in heaps——

HERDA. Edward!

CASS. Edward! Why were you baptized by a doctor? Symbolic? With the arms of your trade, a scalpel and a hypodermic?

(SARCLET *is drinking rather a lot.*)

ABIGAIL (*to* CASS). He's the minister, but he's a doctor, too. Once when someone broke his arm on the Skerry—— (*She stands on the bottom step.*)

HERDA (*quickly*). Edward is suggesting that Stephen go to Longhope for a week.

(ABIGAIL *mounts to the second stair.*)

ABIGAIL. Oh—why?

SARCLET. More sport; you can shoot things there.

ABIGAIL. You can shoot things here, if they don't shoot you first!

CASS. But I'm not going!

ABIGAIL. Longhope is a beautiful place.

CASS. So is this a beautiful place! Like Ulysses I am happy to remain in the Lotus Isle.

(ABIGAIL *drinks.*)

SARCLET. Fill up, fill up!

HERDA. Edward, why do you wish to intoxicate everyone ? Last time there were tears.

ABIGAIL. Last time—there were tears——

SARCLET. Oh, hold your idiotic tongues. I wish to lose my-self and be happy, and I wish my friend to be happy. Don't nag, lady, don't nag . . . (*He refills his glass.*) Ah, I'm beginning to feel happy. It was just that last sip. It was fifty-fifty whether it would make me gloomy or gay . . . I'm *gay* ! (*He turns in the chair, holds up his glass to* CASS *and drinks.*)

(CASS *looks at* SARCLET. ABIGAIL *is watching* CASS. *She is happy too, and she stretches out her hand and touches his. The sudden touch makes him jump and he drops the glass.*)

CASS. Oh !

ABIGAIL. I'm sorry ! Oh, I am sorry !

(*Together they bend to pick up the pieces.*)

SARCLET. Four and sixpence to pay !

HERDA. Leave it, Stephen, I will get a broom. (*She rises.*)

(*A bit of glass enters* CASS'S *glove and the red blood starts oozing through from his hand.*)

ABIGAIL. Oh, Stephen ! Stephen, you're hurt ! Your hand —it's bleeding. Father ! His hand ! (*She kneels on the stairs.*)

(SARCLET *leaps to his feet and strides up stage to* CASS. CASS'S *face suddenly goes grey. He rises and stands at the foot of the stairs with his back to the audience.*)

SARCLET (*to* ABIGAIL.) Hold your noise, girl. Don't start hysterics ! (*He turns to* CASS.) Herda, get my bag !

(HERDA *goes up* R. *to the bookcase.*)

It's only a small cut . . . it's only that. It *can* only be that . . . Now—don't swoon on us, Cassius, be good boy—good boy —only bit of glass.

(HERDA *crosses with the bag to* SARCLET, *opening it as she moves. She holds it for him.* CASS *laughs.* SARCLET *rips off the glove, watching* CASS'S *white face. He takes a piece of bandage from the bag and quickly turns it round the cut. He laughs, suddenly relieved.* CASS *turns down stage.* HERDA *crosses up* R. *with the bag and replaces it on the bookcase.*)

On the morning this happened, it was early, the sun hadn't reached the valleys. I couldn't do very much to help him. "How do you feel, Cassius ? " I said. " Like a hermit crab," he replied, " with someone's foot on my shell " . . . Then he laughed . . . (*He pats* CASS'S *hand.*) Well, you've got your glove off ! . . . Take off the other !

CASS. I can't.

(SARCLET *notes the sweat on* CASS'S *brow.*)

SARCLET. Please yourself . . . That sobered me up, I must have another !—I must have a dozen. (*He turns away.*)

CASS. Take it off for me, Edward. (*He makes a move towards* SARCLET.)

SARCLET. Take it off yourself—— (*He moves down* L. *of the chair* C. *to the tea-table and fills his glass.*)

CASS. I can't.

SARCLET. Yes, you can.

(HERDA *crosses to the foot of the stairs and kneels down to pick up the pieces of glass.*)

ABIGAIL. I'll do it for you, Stephen.

(CASS *turns up to her and, with a smile, holds out his hand.* HERDA *watches.* ABIGAIL *removes the glove.*)

How cold you are—like ice—your hands.

SARCLET (*turning to* HERDA). Not drinking, Herda ?

HERDA (*rising and going to the serving-table*). No, thank you.

(*She puts the pieces of glass on the tray and then comes down between the settee and the chair* C.)

SARCLET. Determined Death's Head at the feast.

HERDA. The feast of what ? (*She sits on the settee.*)

CASS. The Feast of Lanterns——

ABIGAIL. That's a Chinese feast. (*She comes down between the settee and the chair* C. *with her empty glass and refills it.*)

CASS. Is it ? I don't know.

ABIGAIL. How do you know about it if you don't know about it ?

CASS. I don't know . . . I just said it.

ABIGAIL. This is my third—last time I had seven. Miss Tanner had nine and her face was red and shiny. (*She crosses back to* CASS.)

CASS. Who is Miss Tanner ?

ABIGAIL (*softly*). She isn't—she *was* !

(SARCLET *turns towards* ABIGAIL.)

CASS. Was she your governess ?

(CASS *suddenly hears the cry of the kittiwakes.*)

ABIGAIL. No !—She was an actress from London.

CASS. Listen, Herda ! Guy !—Guy !—Guy !

ABIGAIL (*laughing quietly*). Stephen would have liked Guy, wouldn't he, Herda ?

(SARCLET *looks sternly at* ABIGAIL. HERDA *looks up worried.*
*Nobody speaks for a second.*)

SARCLET. Abigail!
ABIGAIL. Guy Clisby!
SARCLET. Abigail!
CASS. Who is Guy Clisby!
SARCLET. Leave the room, Abigail!

(CASS *turns away towards the stairs.*)

HERDA. Edward——
SARCLET (*to* HERDA). You keep out of this. (*To* ABIGAIL.)
Go on, leave the room instantly.

(CASS *looks frowningly at* SARCLET.)

ABIGAIL. I will not. I am twenty-six years old.
SARCLET. I don't care if you're fifty-six. I'm your father,
and you shall obey me.

(ABIGAIL *stands her ground, smiling rather strangely and swaying,*
*the glass in her hand.* HERDA *rises.*)

ABIGAIL. Try and make me!—But you cannot because I am
bigger than you . . . I'm tall and high and happy and you're
—a small man——

(SARCLET *strides towards her.*)

HERDA (*crossing quickly to* ABIGAIL). Come, Abby dear, come
with me, you—— (*She tries to take* ABIGAIL *by the arm.*)

(ABIGAIL *wrenches free and stands on the bottom stair firmly with*
*both feet.*)

ABIGAIL. Stephen! Do you like me as tall as this! Stephen,
I'm nearly as tall as you now, aren't I?
CASS. I never had to look up or down to find your eyes——
SARCLET. Abigail! Leave the room.
ABIGAIL. Stephen! Isn't this exciting!
SARCLET. Abigail!
ABIGAIL. Tell me about . . . Tell me.
SARCLET. Abigail!
HERDA. For heaven's sake, Edward——
ABIGAIL. Oh, Stephen!
HERDA. They're very happy, why break up the celebration?
ABIGAIL. Oh, Stephen—I can feel the clouds round my ankles.
(*She sways slightly.*)
SARCLET. Abby knows.
CASS (*holding out his hands to her*). Hold my hands, Abby—
never let go of my hands——
SARCLET. She has flagrantly disobeyed my wishes.

HERDA.  Oh, well, forget it.

ABIGAIL.  He has been dead for two years, Stephen—two years of rolling mists and sunshine.

CASS.  Dead ?

SARCLET (*crossing to the bear-skin rug*).  Abigail, I warn you not to say that name !

ABIGAIL (*her voice rising*).  Guy Clisby !  Guy Clisby !  Guy Clisby !!  (*She turns on* SARCLET.)

(HERDA *tries to take her arm, but, her eyes blazing, she pushes her off.*)

I'm sick of being treated like a child.  I stopped being a child a hundred years ago——

SARCLET (*turning to* ABIGAIL).  If you don't leave the room I shall carry you out myself.

HERDA.  Come, darling, come.  (*She makes a move to* ABIGAIL.) You know Edward doesn't want you to say any more.

ABIGAIL (*making a move to* CASS).  Guy was a naughty boy . . . he's dead now . . . people don't die, do they, Stephen ?

CASS.  Not if you don't want them to, Abby.

(ABIGAIL *stands regarding him thoughtfully.* HERDA *slips her hand under her arm and with no struggle* ABIGAIL *allows herself to be led upstairs and off.* CASS *stands facing* SARCLET.)

Who was he ? . . .  Who was he ? . . .  Is he the person who plays my music ? . . .  (*He crosses down stage towards* SARCLET.) Very well, Edward, I'll ask Abigail.  (*He returns to the stairs and starts up them.*)

(SARCLET *turns away.*)

SARCLET.  He was hanged for murder.

(CASS *stops on the stairs and turns* L. *to face* SARCLET.)

CASS.  Oh ! . . .  (*There doesn't seem anything else to say. Then :*)  Poor Abigail !  (*He moves down the stairs slowly.*)

SARCLET (*rounding on him*).  Why ?

CASS.  She loved him . . .

SARCLET.  What are you talking about ?

CASS.  You must have known that.  (*He crosses to* SARCLET.)

SARCLET.  She was a child.  A wide-eyed hysterical child.

CASS.  That's the most agonizing love.  Who did he—who— did he——?  What I am trying to say is, who did he—— murder ?

SARCLET.  Miss Tanner—an actress—from London.

CASS.  Why ?

SARCLET.  Really, Cassius, you are as morbid as anyone else when it comes to murders. . . .  It was all in the papers.

CASS  I didn't see it.

SARCLET.  She was going to have a baby.  The kindest thing one can say of him is that he didn't *mean* to kill her too—he was my—all our friend. . . .  I don't like talking about it. . . . D'you mind ? . . .  I feel very annoyed with Abigail for upsetting my Whipcoll. . . .  I wish we'd never come to Skail. I wish we'd gone to Longhope.

(CASS *turns up stage and goes out through the conservatory.* SARCLET *watches him for a moment, then crosses to the* L. *side of the window and stands looking off after him.  Then he comes down to the tea-table and drinks two glasses of Whipcoll slowly and deliberately.*  ABIGAIL *enters down the stairs and stands on the half-landing.*)

Go upstairs !

ABIGAIL.  You are drinking a lot.  (*She comes down the stairs.*)

SARCLET.  Don't come near me——

ABIGAIL.  Och !  I'm away out——  (*She moves towards the window.*)

SARCLET.  Where are you going ?

ABIGAIL.  Out.

SARCLET (*moving quickly to the window and barring the way*). I want to speak to you.

(ABIGAIL *stands looking at him.*)

And you'd better take that insolent expression off your face.

ABIGAIL.  You gave me my face . . . then you changed it— (*she pauses*)—now somebody else has changed it.

SARCLET.  Young lady, you are getting a little beyond yourself.  I thought I forbade you to mention *that name* in this house.

(ABIGAIL *hesitates.  Then :*)

ABIGAIL (*impulsively*).  I'm sorry, Father. . . .  I know what you mean . . . I suddenly felt . . . that it didn't matter any more talking about Guy . . . that it was . . .  We're all older —looking along the road ahead, not glancing back at every step——

SARCLET.  Oh ?  That's exceedingly interesting.  Perhaps we don't—(*he crosses to the fire*)—all of us—change so easily— perhaps, because I am older, I find it less easy to forget my best friend's treachery——

ABIGAIL.  Father . . . (*she moves to the back of the chair* C.) . . . I don't know how to say this to you . . . I don't know you very well . . . I've always been a little afraid of you too . . . but . . . (*She hesitates.*)

SARCLET (*after a pause*).  Go on, go on.  What pearl of wisdom comes now ?

ABIGAIL.  I do like him . . . Stephen . . . I—I want him

so much to like me too. . . . I hope you don't mind. I hope you'll be pleased, because—well, there hasn't been anyone I liked except Guy.

(SARCLET *bursts out laughing.*)

SARCLET. The irony! The scurrilous irony of that!

(ABIGAIL *gazes at him in astonishment.*)

ABIGAIL. What have I said . . .
SARCLET. The laugh's on me!
ABIGAIL. Why do you laugh?
SARCLET. For a variety of reasons, (*he crosses to the piano*) my daughter, firstly the Whipcoll has me in its thrall, and secondly because the biter is bit!—Oh, how the biter is bit! Oh! I should sob and beat the ground for my own stupidity but, oh, no! The Orkney Wizard laughs! Laughs!

(ABIGAIL *looks bewildered ; frightened.*)

(*He turns to her and changes his tone.*) When you were a child you were in love with Guy Clisby . . .
ABIGAIL. Father, that's unfair!
SARCLET. Now you are a woman—(*he goes up to her*)—you are in love with Guy Clisby! Who was it said people always fall in love with the same person?—Oh! Why do I find it so funny, so very, very funny!
ABIGAIL (*aghast*). Father! . . . I've just told you. I'm trying to tell you that it's Stephen—Stephen! Don't laugh like that, you frighten me.

(SARCLET *laughs again, passing his hand across his face. Then solemnly he turns to her.*)

SARCLET (*grabbing her*). Like Macbeth I am reckless what I do to spite the world. I hate everyone, save you, and Stephen. I know I've never shown you the love I ought, a father's love . . . things were wrong for me, Abby . . . your mother and I . . . not even in the same key . . . but I love you . . . I'm proud of you, I feel we're the same flesh, I want you to love me . . . not be frightened like when you were a child, Abby. (*He releases her and moves up towards the stairs.*) When you look at me with those eyes . . . I feel strong . . . I feel I can confide . . . that you'll understand! Not be frightened . . . (*He falls over the stairs.*) Oh, Whipcoll is my undoing! Oh dear, oh dear, I'm very drunk——

(ABIGAIL *moves down below the settee.* SARCLET *shakes his head, trying to collect himself. He comes down to* L. *of the tea-table. She stands immovable before him.*)

Abby . . . you like Stephen?—I'm glad. I like Stephen . . .

love Stephen. He's good. I'm a bad man . . . Abby! (*He moves round the table and seizes her hands suddenly, peering deeply into her eyes.*) Abby! His hands! . . . You don't mind about his hands, do you ? . . . They're good hands . . . strong hands . . . kind hands . . . and soon——

ABIGAIL (*breaking in*). I don't mind . . . I wouldn't mind if he had no hands . . . or no eyes . . . I would be his hands, I would be his eyes.

SARCLET. Abigail! . . . it's not that . . . his hands . . . those hands! . . . You've seen them before!

(ABIGAIL *stares at him, not understanding.*)

Abigail! Don't look at me like that. . . . Look, I'll tell you, you're a grown-up young lady now, aren't you ? I can talk to you! . . . and you can understand and . . . say—it's all right —and——

ABIGAIL. What's all right ? . . . What's all right ? . . . What's all right ?

SARCLET. Stephen . . . Guy Clisby . . . their hands . . . are . . . the same . . . Abby—I gave Guy's hands—to Stephen!—Abby!

(*For a second she stands staring, eyes wide, mouth hanging open foolishly, her body swaying in the air like a marionette on a string. . . . Then she throws back her head and bursts into a peal of mad laughter. He takes a step towards her as she falls senseless to the ground.*)

CURTAIN.

SCENE 2

SCENE.—*The same. That night.*
    *The wind has risen and the Orkney night is darker than it should be by reason of the heavy mist which is blowing inshore.*

HERDA *enters through the archway* L. *She crosses to the* C. *window and pulls apart the curtains and peers out.* SARCLET *enters through the archway* L. *He is coming from the dining-room and lights a cigar as he enters. He looks at* HERDA. HERDA *leaves the window and comes down* R. SARCLET *crosses to the fireplace and inhales deeply.*

SARCLET. I'm glad you lit the fire. It's cold enough.
HERDA (*sitting in the chair down* R.). It's you who are cold.

(*She takes her work off the work-table and starts sewing. Every now and then, through the ensuing dialogue, her fingers stop work and she looks up and listens for the sound of footsteps—then sighing deeply resumes her work.*)

SARCLET. Why should I be cold if you are not ? *I'm* not a cold-blooded, sexless frog. (*He moves up to the window.*)

HERDA. Your conscience could make you cold, leaving a young girl out in these dangerous mists.

SARCLET (*irritably*). Are you going to start that puritanical nonsense again ! *I did not leave her out. She went out——* (*He comes down to the chair* c. *and sits.*)

(HERDA *doesn't answer.*)

The girl knows her way about Skail after twenty-six years . . . you've never shown the least anxiety before.

HERDA. Once . . .

SARCLET. That was an occasion for hysterics too I remember.

HERDA. She's very highly strung and emotional just now. She's not in a fit state to be wandering about.

SARCLET. She's perfectly well able to look after herself. She knows the surroundings considerably better than any of us. Now if it were I out there scaling the skerries you'd have reason for despair——

HERDA. What makes you think so ?

SARCLET. Rude too, I see——

HERDA. You should have gone with Cass to look for her.

SARCLET. Cass said he was only going to the beach. She was in the room, I went into the garden——

HERDA. Why ?

SARCLET. I felt sick . . . when I came back she had gone.

HERDA. Listen !——

SARCLET. That's Cass now. (*He rises, crosses to the fire and turns towards* c., *looking at the window.*)

(*Footsteps come up to the window and it opens. CASS stands there alone. He looks pale and worried, the rose in his buttonhole is crushed and dead. He is wearing his Inverness. After a moment he comes into the room and closes the window.*)

CASS. I've called and called !—I've climbed the skerry—it was wet and I didn't know where I was. . . . Yet I know she's on the skerry—I don't know why she won't answer me—— (*He crosses to the piano.*)

HERDA (*rising and going to* SARCLET ; *her sewing in her hands*). Edward ! You *must* go now ! Maybe she's hurt——

SARCLET. Don't be absurd !—I don't know why you are both making such a——

HERDA. She hasn't been back since this morning ! It's not like her to remain away when we have visitors ! Edward, *please* !—Stephen ! Make him go——

SARCLET. *Make* me go ?

CASS. I shall go. (*He moves to* c.)

HERDA. No. Edward must go——

SARCLET. I'm not going out. Once and for all. I've changed my shoes. (*He goes up to the window.*)

CASS. I'll go again, Herda. I want to find her—— (*He moves up to the window.*)

SARCLET (*removing* CASS's *cape*). *I forbid you to!* You don't know the way and you're in no state. (*He hangs the cape over the balustrade.*)

HERDA. Neither is Abby! I shall go myself. (*She moves down to the work-table and puts her work down on it.*)

SARCLET (*to* CASS). Sit down and pull yourself together, and if you'll take my advice you'll go to bed, Cassius. So will you, Herda. You're behaving like a maniac.

CASS (*turning down to the chair* C.). No, I'd rather wait till she comes in.

HERDA. Edward—supposing something *has* happened . . . she has slipped . . . hurt herself.

SARCLET (*wearily*). Stop fussing for another hour. . . . If she hasn't returned by midnight, wake me up and I'll go and look for her, though how I should be able to find her or know where to look——

HERDA. I think you're very heartless. I think you're afraid.

SARCLET. Afraid! Of what?

HERDA. The dark!

(SARCLET *turns away towards the stairs.*)

SARCLET (*going up the stairs*). No, it's cupboards on stairs that I'm afraid of. Good night, Cassius.

(*He continues up the stairs and off.* CASS *and* HERDA *do not reply.* HERDA *crosses to* CASS.)

HERDA. Stephen, go up to bed, you look so tired and pale. I shall wait another hour, as Edward suggests, and then I shall wake him and force him out.

CASS. You're worried, aren't you?

HERDA. Well, it's true, as Edward says, that no one knows the district better and she has often been away by herself all day . . . (*she crosses to the fire-stool and sits*) but I don't think she would do such a thing when you are here.

CASS. She'll be back soon, I *know*, and in the meanwhile I'll stay with you. I should like that. (*He crosses to the settee, at the* L. *end, and drops into it.*)

(HERDA *rises, moves to the* R. *end of the settee and sits.* CASS *settles himself down, crossing one leg over the other thoughtfully, then he looks down at his hands.*)

HERDA. What are you looking at?

CASS (*with a smile*). The hands of a man I should have liked to know.

HERDA.  What a strange, wonderful thing Edward did for you.  I can forgive him his heartlessness tonight when I think of them.

CASS.  Your brother—he's a very strange man.

(*For a second* HERDA *doesn't reply.*)

HERDA.  Do you have much pain now ?

CASS.  Not much, not any more.  I suffer most from that Italian malady of the heart called " *Smara* " !

HERDA.  *Smara ?*—I never heard of it——

CASS.  Disquietude——

HERDA.  You remind me of Karel Capek's pilgrim who doesn't know where he's going but who does not journey in vain.

CASS (*quietly*).  Did Abigail love Clisby ?

(HERDA *is surprised.*)

HERDA.  We all did—he lived here—they were brought up together as children—he taught her to fish and climb the skerries —I used to wash his hair.

CASS.  And Miss Tanner from London . . . where does she come into the picture ?

HERDA.  He met her in London.  You see, Stephen, since he grew up he had become a great traveller, he travelled all over the world . . . there—there had been " Miss Tanners " everywhere.  Abby was too " young " for him—too untramelled.  He was older . . . he was more Edward's friend ; knew the same kind of people, had the same jokes.  (*She pauses.*)  Miss Tanner was a well-known beauty . . . an actress, and amusing . . . he brought her up here to his house—the little one on the edge of the Bay—the Islands didn't like her, she didn't speak softly and she laughed at everything—Abby included.  That really broke Abby's heart more than anything else, I think ! . . .  But she had never really known Guy since he grew up—it was a good thing there was a Miss Tanner, for he used to sit and stare at Abby—and it would never have done—never—never.

CASS.  What was he like ?  Tell me about him.

HERDA.  There was something awfully " fine " about him as a boy that somehow never left him . . . he was proud like a tree, he——

CASS.  Why did he do it ?

HERDA.  No one quite knew why he did it . . . he—he tried to defend himself at the trial . . . but at the end—it seemed there was too much against him—so he just laughed.

CASS.  Laughed !  A man doesn't give away his life so easily.

HERDA.  Edward told me that.  He went out of the court-room laughing. . . .  He used to laugh a lot, I remember. . . .

CASS.  How much does she know ?

HERDA.  Everything.

CASS.  And what was everything ?
HERDA.  Oh dear——

(CASS *doesn't help her—just waits for her to go on.*)

Well, Guy had been away, it appeared—when he came back
Miss Tanner met him as usual, apparently very gay—he—they
—went back to her rooms and in the morning when he woke she
was dead—poisoned.
CASS.  Where did the poison come from ?
HERDA.  Some was found in Guy's rooms which he shared
with Edward, but unfortunately Edward couldn't help him in
any way because Edward had been away too, in Paris at that
time.
CASS.  Was there an autopsy taken ?
HERDA.  Yes——
CASS.  *Any* possible motive for murder shown ?
HERDA (*after a pause*).  She—she was going to have a baby.
CASS.  She might have poisoned herself.
HERDA.  That was something nobody could prove—and then
finding the poison in Guy's room made things black for him—
it was some new drug.
CASS.  Oh ?
HERDA.  All the circumstances—everything was against him
all the way, and his reputation didn't help either.

(*There is a pause.*)

CASS.  Poor Guy.
HERDA.  Yes.  (*She turns away.*)
CASS (*after a pause*).  Poor Abigail.

(*There is something about his voice that makes* HERDA *look up.*)

HERDA.  Forgive me, but—you love her, don't you ?

(CASS *doesn't answer but turns away, a smile about his lips.*)

Oh, Stephen, you don't have to say a word—how lucky she
is——
CASS.  But there are always these !  (*He turns to her and
holds up his hands with a little laugh.*)
HERDA.  What difference do they make ?
CASS.  They have made me an unpleasant person to live with,
nervy and short-tempered and restless.  You never told my
fortune, Herda !—Look at my hands and tell me how many
children I have !

(*His expression changes suddenly, his eyes widening as he looks at
her, realizing what he has said.  Then he drops his hands into
his lap and sits hunched up.*)

HERDA (*after a pause*).  It isn't really in the hands, you know

Stephen, that you read! It's something more than that . . . I know a lot of things about you, but I would know them without looking at your hands . . . there's not much future in a hand, it's character—illness, mental strain in the past . . . not how many children a man shall have! Come, give me your hand and I will tell you a little about—*him*.

(CASS *holds his hand up to her; she looks at it closely, turning it about.*)

There are only three clearly defined lines . . . here is a direct, generous, calm character, humorous—not very happy, not very unhappy—lonely, seeking adventure; musical . . . about your age. (*She frowns, peering closer.*) Did you make those marks?

(CASS *too peers closely.*)

CASS. Those four deep little scars, you mean?—No, they look like nail marks, don't they, as if someone had clenched his hands tightly, in anger, or fear. I often look at them.

HERDA. Strange——

CASS. I find I do it too—it's another of my unpleasant habits!

HERDA (*suddenly listening*). That's Abigail! (*She rises quickly and moves round the* R. *end of the settee to above it.*)

(*They both listen.* CASS *rises and moves to the fireplace. Footsteps are heard in the conservatory and a moment later the window opens and* ABIGAIL *stands there. She comes in, closing the window behind her. Her hair is covered with mist that sparkles on her head and her lashes like jewelled tears, but her face is pale and lifeless, and she stares straight at* CASS *without speaking.*)

(*As she goes up to* ABIGAIL'S R.) Abby, my darling! We have been so worried, Stephen and I—where have you been? Poor Stephen went out and called your name.

ABIGAIL. I heard. (*She comes to the back of the chair* C. *She still stares at* CASS.)

CASS. You—heard—and you didn't answer——

HERDA. Abby! (*She comes down to her.*) How unkind of you not to answer and save us worry! . . . Why have you been away so long, darling? You're wet too, let Herda take off your jacket. (*She helps her off with her coat, then takes it into the conservatory, puts it off* L. *and returns.*)

(CASS *and* ABIGAIL *stare at each other.*)

CASS. You wanted—you wanted to escape from me?

HERDA (*coming down to the back of the settee,* L. *end*). Stephen, why should she?

CASS. She heard my " wild entreaties "! . . . She didn't

answer, did she ? . . . What is it, Abby ?—Why do you look at me like that ?—As if you'd seen a ghost——

(ABIGAIL *only stares.*)

HERDA. Never mind now, Stephen. She's tired. Tomorrow everything will be different . . . (*To* ABIGAIL.) Come, let's all go to bed, it's late. (*She takes a step towards her.*)

ABIGAIL. That rose is dead. You should throw it away— it's no use keeping things when they're dead—" lilies that fester smell far worse than weeds."

HERDA. Abby dear——

CASS (*moving towards her, two steps*). Can I get you something to drink ? Milk ? Or tea ?

HERDA. Abby, dear, some warm milk ? Stephen will get it for you, it would do you good, wouldn't it ?

(ABIGAIL *can only stare at* CASS *and he at her.*)

CASS. I'll go. I know where everything is.

(*He crosses to* L. *and goes out through the archway. He seems in a hurry and has gone before* HERDA *can speak.*)

HERDA. Darling—what is it ? Why are you so strange and where have you been ? Or would you rather tell me tomorrow ?

ABIGAIL. Oh, Herda, how can I bear it.

HERDA. What !—What ?

ABIGAIL (*clutching her*). You must promise me never to leave me. I couldn't bear it if you did.

HERDA. Of course I won't.

ABIGAIL. Herda . . . (*She clasps her hands together tightly.*) We must go away from here, you and I . . . tomorrow . . . early . . . we must go where no one can find us . . . we must go and—and forget.

HERDA. Abby !—What are you talking about ! What is this strange girl ? You frighten me !

ABIGAIL. I'll tell you, only promise to go away with me tomorrow early, before anyone is awake !

HERDA. Things are not so easy as that . . . arrangements— and there's your father.

ABIGAIL. I hope I never see him again. (*She moves away down* L.C. *and then across to* C.)

HERDA. Oh, Abby ! Abby ! What has happened ? (*She takes a step down between the chair* C. *and the settee.*)

ABIGAIL (*turning up to the chair* C. *and kneeling in it ; in quick tones*). It was Father . . . he told me . . . something . . . (*She licks her dry lips. She is facing* R.) He didn't mean to tell me, I don't think . . . it was the Whipcoll made him do it . . . the Viking drink that spoilt my life before when that foreign woman laughed at me and spilled her drink down her blouse——

HERDA.  What did he tell you ?  (*She is facing directly down stage.*)

ABIGAIL.  About Stephen——

HERDA.  About Stephen? What about Stephen! You mustn't believe anything you hear about Stephen so easily.

(CASS *appears in the archway.  He is walking carefully, so as not to upset the milk.  The dead rose has gone from his coat.*)

ABIGAIL.  It was something dreadful about Stephen . . . something I can never forget . . . a terrible, terrible something ; and that's why we must go away, you and I, so that Stephen never finds out, for I think it would destroy him too if he knew.

(CASS *pauses in the archway, not knowing what to do.*)

HERDA.  Oh, what !

ABIGAIL.  He said . . . the laugh was on him . . . and the biter was bit . . . he said that Stephen . . . Stephen and Guy . . . had the same hands ! . . . Stephen's hands, Herda ! They're Guy's ! They're Guy's ! . . . Father took Guy's hands and gave them to Stephen ! Oh, how could he ! How could he do that to us all !

(CASS *is like a carven figure, rigid.  HERDA stares at ABIGAIL, speechless, then in a whisper :*)

HERDA.  How can I bear it for you !

(ABIGAIL *turns suddenly and sees CASS.  His eyes look black in the pale drawn face ; destroyed, crushed by what he has heard.  For a second they look at each other—then with a funny little movement of his face he holds out the glass of warm milk.  With an indrawn sob ABIGAIL speeds up the stairs.  HERDA doesn't know what to do or say, she can't move from where she is standing, unable to remove her eyes from that stricken face.  He doesn't seem to see her, doesn't seem to see anything.  A little frown runs across his brow and unconsciously, nervously, he starts picking at his fingers.  HERDA hurries towards the stairs.  As she comes level with him she takes the glass of milk out of his hand.  He sees her and smiles, like a child who doesn't want you to know where it's been hurt ; then the smile fades, leaving the face blank as before. HERDA puts out her hand and takes his.  She puts her lips to the back of it.  Then she runs up the stairs to ABIGAIL.  CASS stands where she has left him.  He holds out his hands looking at them ; then hopelessly, he drops them limply to his side.*)

SLOW CURTAIN.

## SCENE 3

SCENE.—*The same. Early the following morning.*
*There is no colour in the sky and the room is almost dark.*
*The clock strikes four.*

CASS *is sitting in front of the fire. He is thinking. After a*
*moment he rises, crosses to the window and peers out, his hands*
*behind his back ; then, turning, he moves to the stairs and looks*
*up and along them. He is evidently waiting for someone. He*
*returns to the window, opens it and steps out through the con-*
*servatory.* ABIGAIL *enters quickly down the stairs. She carries*
*a lamp. She hesitates for a moment on the upper stairs looking*
*down into the room to make sure no one is about. She is dressed*
*for a journey and carries a small portmanteau in her hand. She*
*comes down the remainder of the stairs and goes out through the*
*archway* L. *A second later* HERDA *enters down the stairs. She*
*too carries a lamp and a portmanteau and is dressed for travelling.*
*She goes out through the archway* L. *Almost immediately the*
*two women return, having deposited their cases. They are talking*
*in undertones.*

ABIGAIL (*entering ; anxiously*). How long will Fletty be with
the wagon then ? (*She crosses to the window.*)

HERDA (*following her*). As soon as she can. Don't be
impatient.

ABIGAIL. But I do not wish to see anyone, least of all Edward
Sarclet. (*She catches sight of* CASS *in the garden.*) Oh ! (*She*
*clutches* HERDA'S *arm.*) Stephen's up ! (*She turns to* HERDA.)
We won't be able to get away without seeing him. (*She crosses*
HERDA *to the serving-table and puts her lamp on it.*)

HERDA. I think it would be exceedingly unkind if you did.
After all, he must have heard most of the conversation and I
should have thought you——

ABIGAIL. No ! No ! I don't want to see him. (*She moves*
*to the foot of the stairs.*)

HERDA (*going to her ; with an attempt at a smile*). Afraid
you'll change your mind ?

ABIGAIL (*disregarding this last*). Let's go and sit in the kitchen
until the wagon arrives.

HERDA. I want to leave a note for Edward. It's only right
that we should do so. I shall go and write a note to him in his
study. You may go to the kitchen if you wish to, and I will
join you later. (*Rather noisily, she is suddenly attacked with a*
*sneezing fit.*)

(ABIGAIL *looks alarmed.* HERDA *gives a sidelong look towards the*
*garden and hurries out through the archway* L. CASS *comes to*
*the window.* ABIGAIL *is just about to follow* HERDA *when his*
*voice arrests her.*)

CASS. Abigail! (*He steps in and stands up* C.)

(ABIGAIL *stops dead in her track. She does not turn.*)

Don't turn round.  Just listen to what I have to say.  I've been awake all night after hearing what you told Herda.  I knew too that you would be leaving early this morning.  Abby . . . Abby, don't go!

(ABIGAIL *doesn't move.*)

You don't turn your face to me because you can't bear to look at me . . . but if I told you that I——

ABIGAIL. No!

CASS. You can't look at me because you still love Clisby?

(ABIGAIL *doesn't answer.*)

Or because you are repulsed by the thought of my touch?

(*Still* ABIGAIL *cannot answer, but her eyes close as though the question were agony to her.*)

If it is the first, you need never fear my intrusion . . . if it is the last, then no matter where you hide yourself, my darling, one day I will come and find you . . . the right day . . . when everything will be right.

(ABIGAIL *doesn't move.*)

Turn, Abby . . . turn . . . smile . . . the hands are safe behind my back.  I will not move from where I stand . . . only let me see your face . . . my face . . . Abby?

(ABIGAIL *gathers herself together and turns.  They look at each other.*)

Worlds, years between us . . . you on one shore and me on the other! . . .  I never saw you in a hat . . . nor trout fishing . . . nor waving from the valley . . . nor in a London street . . . nor quietly opposite me at a table for two with the candle glimmering between . . . but how near I always was to you. Twice we almost met, but once you crossed the street too soon and once I rang the bell too late!

(ABIGAIL *says nothing, her eyes dark and enormous in her pale, beautiful face.  In silence they stare at each other again as though drinking in something they each wished to remember. Then* CASS *smiles.  She still stands looking at him, her lower lip caught in her teeth, then she turns and rushes out through the archway* L.  *He stands where she has left him, not attempting to follow.  Outside on the gravel in the front of the house, a wagon draws up and women's voices come to him faintly through closed doors.  He remains, moving not at all.  The wagon moves off, the horses' hooves breaking into a trot as they near the iron gateway,*

*and then fade into silence. Still he never moves. Now there is
no sound anywhere.* SARCLET *enters down the stairs. His hair
is unbrushed and he wears a woollen dressing-gown and carries
his black bag.*)

SARCLET (*entering*). Pandebloodymonium! I am resuscitated
from a dream about the garden of the Hesperides, to find hideous
day full of the sound of cackling women and cantering hooves.
What is going on? In my half sleep I flung on my robe, snatched
my medical bag and made for the stairs, certain that my brilliant
brain was needed. (*He reaches the bottom of the stairs.*)

CASS. It is.

SARCLET. Ah . . . who is in trouble? (*He puts his bag on
the downstage end of the serving-table.*)

CASS. You are, my dear Edward. They have gone. (*He
comes down to the back of the chair* C.)

SARCLET. Gone? Who have?

CASS. Your sister and your daughter.

SARCLET. What do you mean? Gone where? To Kirk-
wall? Why?

CASS. I don't know where they've gone. They didn't propose
to tell me. They have just gone. Each wore travelling clothes
and carried a portmanteau.

(*There is a pause.*)

SARCLET (*astounded*). Gone? Left?

(SARCLET *crosses to the archway* L. *and goes out calling.*)

Herda! Abigail!

(*There is silence. A moment later he reappears carrying a note.
He looks at* CASS.)

They *have* gone!

CASS. Do they say where? *And why?*

SARCLET. This is from Herda. She says—why. (*He stands
staring at* CASS, *flicking the paper with his fingers, not knowing
what goes next.*)

CASS. I know why too.

SARCLET (*crossing to the serving-table*). Oh . . . (*He pours
out a drink.*)

CASS. I overheard Abigail tell Herda last night. I went to
get the milk.

SARCLET. The milk—yes. Oh . . . (*He moves down between
the chair* C. *and the settee and sits in the chair.*)

(*Neither of them speaks for some moments.*)

CASS. I have had all night to think of it . . . now I'm watching you go through it too, but it won't be the same for you
because I was thinking of her . . . and you are thinking of
Edward Sarclet.

SARCLET.  Quite right—quite right.

CASS.  Why did you have to tell her ?  And if you told her so easily why didn't you tell me ?  God knows I've been asking you to for two years !  I should have waited a bit longer, waited for that last ounce of Whipcoll to be drunk.

SARCLET.  You're becoming almost insulting, Cassius.

CASS.  I'm just the smallest bit angry !

SARCLET.  Oh, don't be a fool.  (*He rises and turns to* L.C.)  My home crashes about my ears, my sister and my daughter rushing away in wagons in the early hours of the morning, leaving notes not telling where they're going . . . and you dare to be the smallest bit angry !

(CASS *laughs at the effrontery of this.*)

CASS.  By God, you really are the world's megalomaniac !

SARCLET.  If they think I'm going after them—they're right.

(*He turns up to the stairs.*  CASS *steps in front of him and stops him.*)

CASS.  No.

SARCLET.  Leave me alone.  D'you think I'm going to allow a couple of geese about by themselves ?

CASS.  You weren't thinking of that.  You were still thinking of Edward Sarclet.  You're afraid.

SARCLET.  Afraid ?  Ha !  What should I have to fear from two foolish women ?

CASS.  Afraid they'll spoil something for you.  The only person who is likely to do that—is here, now, in the room with you.

(SARCLET *looks at him.*)

SARCLET.  What do you mean ?

CASS.  I have the right to tell the world that you have made me the proud possessor of murderer's hands !  After all, I may want to conciliate myself with the *police* in the event of the unforeseen habits I may have collected from my predecessor getting the better of me !

SARCLET.  You can tell anyone ! . . .  The operation is a success, the medical profession wouldn't give a hang about such a detail.

CASS.  Edward, you and I are bandying about with words of no value . . . you gave me hands where I would have had stumps, albeit stumps of honour !  The rest of the story need never have been told, had you never brought me to the Orkneys.  That was unforgivable and damnable !

SARCLET.  Why do you talk so much, Cassius ?  Why don't you shut up ?  (*He crosses* CASS *and moves to the serving-table. He refills his glass and drinks.*)

(CASS *watches him.*)

CASS. Now shall we have the rest of the story ?

(*The whisky on the empty stomach has hit the right spot, and* SARCLET *turns on him truculently.*)

SARCLET. Tell the world then ! You can't hurt me ! I'm a success ! Nothing succeeds like success !

CASS. And your family, what are you going to do about them ? About your daughter ?

SARCLET. Let them look after themselves. They'll soon know what it's like to have to earn their living, like my father. . . . They'll never be the man he was. (*He takes another drink.*)

CASS. What are you drinking all that for ?

SARCLET. It's mine. Besides, I'm giving myself an anæsthetic.

CASS. What for ?

SARCLET (*coming down to the tea-table*). I'm going to take off your hands—I don't like them. I'm sick of them, they've caused me a lot of trouble one way or another, they must be thrown in the sea or buried deep where no one can see them. (*He stands down* R. *of the table and faces* CASS.) Don't be frightened of me, Cassius, don't be frightened !

CASS (*facing* SARCLET). I'm not frightened, Edward. I have never been that ; sorry, I have been ; and in a strange way have even loved you ; but frightened, of you . . . never !

SARCLET. . . . Frightened of . . . someone else ? Something ?

CASS. Frightened is an ugly word which one endeavours not to use ! . . . But I have been—perturbed, in mortal funk, sometimes, because you wouldn't tell me what I knew.

SARCLET. Knew ? What did you know ?

CASS. That the man whose hands I had, died with remonstrance on his lips.

SARCLET. That could be said of many—almost all perhaps !

CASS. They were not hands folded quietly in sleep. They trembled and shook, they beat against a wall. They clenched and unclenched. The marks of the nails are still there. (*He looks through the window at the dawn breaking.*)

SARCLET. What are you yattering about ?

CASS. They stretched out suddenly to touch beauty, delighting in the feel of grass, the bark of trees, stone walls warmed by the sun, and rocks where the seaweed lies.

SARCLET. You're trying to intimidate me with your bulging head of poetry  He wasn't any of those things—he was afraid of *me* !

CASS. He was never afraid of you—that man . . . he was not afraid of any man, not even of death . . . for two years I have learned to know him, to respect, like and admire . . . that music, somehow I knew it was his . . . poetry too, we argued about, he and I . . . places and people we liked and disliked together . . . we even liked you, for the better part that we knew. . . . And she, we both loved . . . and now ! . . . Now ! You tell me my friend is a murderer ! (*He comes down to* L. *of the tea-table.*) At first the shock was so great I thought . . . but now, it's all right . . . he didn't mean murder . . . it was a mistake. . . . He loved life, that man . . . he wanted all things to live . . . he was carried along by the Force that was life . . . tell me that ! Tell me what I say is true.

(SARCLET *has never taken his eyes off* CASS, *nor his lips off the glass. He leans across the table.*)

SARCLET. I hate life . . . you like life. Clisby . . . he liked life. Yes . . . (*He smiles sadly.*) Yet you both like me . . . and I am not life. I know more about death. I know more about how to die than how to live. Tell me something . . . tell me why you both like me.

CASS. Don't try and throw me off, Edward. I want your answer. Tell me what I say is true.

SARCLET. Tell me about life.

CASS. Tell me what I say is true.

SARCLET. Tell me about life first . . . then I'll tell anything and everything. (*He moves up between the settee and the chair* C. *to the stairs.*) What is life—Cassius . . . what is it ? (*He sits on the second stair at the* L. *end.*)

CASS (*in spite of himself*). Life—is a cycle of events . . .

SARCLET. Go on.

CASS (*turning to* SARCLET). Edward ! Listen—there are things to do. Abby——

SARCLET (*roaring*). Look, Stephen—go on ! Go on about life ! . . . You're a poet, aren't you ! I'm drunk and I want to know about life.

CASS. Tell me the answer to my question then. Tell me Clisby's murder was a mistake.

SARCLET. What is life ? What is it ?

(*There is a pause.* CASS *crosses to* SARCLET. *He sits on the third stair.*)

CASS. You said yesterday it was waiting, I said it was opportunity. Today it's a Cycle of Events, Edward. Happiness ! Desperation ! Ecstasy ! Despair ! . . . When you're young you can handle the thought of it, when you're old your heart breaks. Was Clisby's murder a mistake, Edward ?

(SARCLET *clutches at his heart and then :*)

SARCLET. I am old . . . my heart broke when I was young because no one believed in me, Cassius. . . . I love you, like the son I never had.

CASS. You haven't answered my question yet, Edward.

SARCLET (*strongly*). What do you want ?

CASS. I want the information you owe me. (*He holds up his hands.*)

SARCLET (*after a pause*). They're as clean as a child's . . . just muddy with adventure.

CASS. I knew !—I knew ! (*He rises and comes to the back of the chair c.*)

SARCLET. *Wait !* (*A slow, devilish smile creeps across his face —a sudden exultation.*)

(CASS *turns to* SARCLET, *surprised by his tone.*)

If you want to lift a stone and look underneath you must expect to find things crawling about. . . . A woman, for instance, with ruddy cheeks and hair curling at the nape of her neck . . . a passionate obstinate woman . . . I used to go round to the theatre to see her when Clisby was away, and take her back to our rooms for supper. She had come there often enough with Clisby, why not with me ? She was like a cat the way she stretched out and yawned and showed her provocative little tongue and tantalizing claws ! (*His tone changes.*) She came to me one day and said she was going to have a child and that it was mine. I told her she couldn't label it mine, but she said she would, and remembering that provocative little tongue I gave her something to take . . . then I went to Paris. Next day Clisby returned and two mornings later he awoke to find her dead beside him. (*He shrugs his shoulders.*) It was unfortunate . . . she took too much—and that left difficulties. Someone had to explain and someone had to be blamed.

CASS. You ?

SARCLET (*shaking his head*). I had a destiny . . . Clisby was just a rolling stone . . . I went to Vogespiegel . . .

(CASS *backs above the chair c. and sits on the settee. He can only stare and stare at* SARCLET.)

Well ? There it is ! My confession ! My two-year-old secret which I have told to my two-year-old friend Cassius ! . . . What is he going to do about it ?

(CASS *continues to stare ; the enormity of it rushing through his mind.*)

Jump to his feet and call me a cad ! . . . Or give me in charge and see me behind bars . . . ? Rather unkind, don't you think ? Rather cruel to the girl he loves ! Don't you think so, Cassius ? . . . Those long fingers and raised eyebrows pointing after her wherever she goes ! . . . And children ! . . . Little murderers, perhaps ! . . . Think of that, my dear boy !

(CASS *never takes his eyes off* SARCLET'S *face.* SARCLET *pauses. He rises and crosses above the chair c. to* CASS.)

Perhaps you see now how foolish you were to dabble. When the poison is quiescent we let it lie. (*He turns back to the serving-table.*) Stimulation produces discoloration. Oh, what a hornet's nest you raised when you lifted that stone ! (*He fills his glass.*)

(CASS *makes a hard little dry sound in his throat that might be a laugh.*)

Well, what does that signify ? (*He turns to* CASS.)

CASS.   You've set me quite a problem, Edward.

SARCLET.   You should at least show joy that your hands are not a murderer's.

CASS.   That joy seems obliterated by the fact that yours are ! And that Abigail is your daughter—quite a little food for thought, Edward. (*He rises and moves to the fireplace.*) However . . . (*He stands staring down into the fire.*)

(SARCLET *watches him covertly.*)

I shall tell her, I shall find her and tell her what you have told me . . . and then——

SARCLET.   Then ?

(CASS *shrugs his shoulders.*)

CASS.   Go away, perhaps . . . for a time.

SARCLET.   Where ?

CASS.   God knows . . . anywhere.

SARCLET.   What about me ?

CASS (*turning*).   You ?—I don't suppose I shall see you again, Edward . . . I don't somehow think I shall care to !

SARCLET.   I suppose you are worried about your soul !

CASS.   My soul is a little out at the elbows—— (*He crosses to the stairs and starts up them.*)

SARCLET.   Wait !

(CASS *turns on the second stair.*)

You have something of mine that I want before you go.

CASS.   Something of yours ?

SARCLET (*coming down to the chair* c.).   Your hands . . .

(CASS *looks astonished, then he laughs.*)

CASS (*seriously*).   They belong to me now. You can't take presents back, you know. You should have learnt that in your nursery ! (*He comes down the stairs and moves slowly towards* SARCLET.)

SARCLET (*shouting*).   Stand still !

(CASS *stops.* SARCLET *turns up to the serving-table and, angrily making odd noises to himself, feverishly opens his medical bag and takes out a hypodermic which he hurriedly fills with some-thing from a phial.*)

CASS. Don't be a fool!

(SARCLET *looks up. Things are not going as he wished. His eyes are red with rage and whisky. He advances on* CASS *with the hypodermic.*)

Put that down, Edward! I want to get that boat for Thurso—Abigail will be there.

(*Still* SARCLET *advances.*)

Your hand is very unsteady, Edward—you need another drink.

SARCLET. I shall drink afterwards—a long cool draught of elixir vitæ.

CASS. There's poison in that for you, Edward.

SARCLET (*moving towards him*). I am Mithridates.

CASS. Even Mithridates slipped. Come, Edward, I want to catch a boat.

SARCLET. Not this tide. You're going to sleep . . .

CASS (*interrupting*). Edward, get out of my way.

(SARCLET *suddenly leans forward and slaps his face.* CASS *goes crimson with anger, his hands flying up to protect his face.*)

(*Quietly.*) Why did you do that?

SARCLET. Take that ugly look off your face.

CASS. I feel ugly. I feel very ugly listening to your dirty little story . . .

(SARCLET'S *face changes.* CASS'S *eyes are unnaturally big and bright. His hands remain in front of his face like great claws.* SARCLET *hesitates.*)

For two years there has been no peace. Someone . . . something always at my elbow urging me on—I never knew where. Troubled and weary, I wandered from place to place, blinded by day, sightless by night . . . on, on, asking, listening, searching, wondering, waiting for the moment that must come when I should know . . . waiting—for this.

SARCLET. Cassius . . .

(SARCLET'S *eyes are riveted on the white talons a few feet from his face.*)

Cass! What are you trying to do? Kill me?

CASS. Now I know . . . now I know—— (*He advances slowly on* SARCLET.)

SARCLET (*backing up* C.). Listen to me, please——

CASS. Now I know. I was looking for you . . . and you were beside me!

(*He continues to advance. He backs* SARCLET *between the settee and the chair* C. *The whites of his eyes frighten* SARCLET, *and his voice as he lifts it suddenly to someone out there beyond the Bay.)*

Clisby! Clisby! This was what you wanted! This was what you wanted!

*(There is a sudden laugh ; a single note of laughter from someone ; a man's laugh. To* CASS *it is unfamiliar, but to* SARCLET *it is enough to make him go ashen and clutch at his heart.)*

SARCLET *(backing in front of the settee towards the fireplace).* Clisby! . . . He laughed . . . Cassius! Cassius! I'm going mad! I heard him laugh! No, no, Cass, don't look at me like that! I'll do anything you like . . . Go away! Go away, Cassius . . . go away!

CASS. I can't, Edward. I can't.

*(*CASS's *hands have the strange and horrifying appearance of being dragged away from his body by some unseen force. And* CASS's *face looks queer, almost stupid, like a child who is being pulled along by a relentless grown-up.)*

SARCLET *(panting).* Cass!—I feel . . . bad, Cass. *(He is getting his breath with difficulty. His hands are clutching at his breast, tearing at the dressing-gown, waving impotently, trying to ward off this oncoming horror of those familiar hands.)* Cass, go away! Cass, I am dying—go away!

CASS. I can't . . . I can't! . . . I can't!

*(Nearer they come, those hands, jerking and craning towards* SARCLET's *face. He closes his eyes, his head drops backwards. Opening his mouth he draws in his breath heavily, noisily; with a moan. Then, like a stone, he falls backwards to the floor. The hands plunge towards him, stiff and rigid. All of a sudden they collapse at the wrist like moonflowers at dawn. . . .* CASS *takes a step to the fireplace where* SARCLET *is lying. He calls softly.)*

Edward! Edward!

*(He stoops over* SARCLET *and touches him ; then draws back and straightens up. He moves slowly to* C. *His eyes fill with tears and he sobs. Then he looks up and down at his hands. He tears his gloves off and throws them down on the floor. He looks at them. Then :)*

*(Looking up.)* Guy! It's all over now. It's all over . . . rest . . . rest now . . . rest . . . *(He turns and moves slowly up to the window and into the conservatory. He looks up. The morning sun catches him. The gulls wheel and scream.)* Abigail!

SLOW CURTAIN.

# NORWEGIAN LOVE SONG

# BOAT SONG

Francis Hayley Bell

# BOAT SONG Off-stage

# FURNITURE AND PROPERTY PLOT

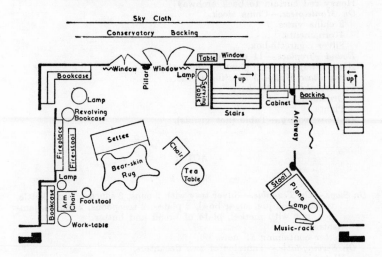

## THROUGHOUT THE PLAY

*On Stage.*—Settee.
    2 armchairs.
    Round tea-table.
    Work-table.
    Long fire-stool.
    Footstool.
    Serving-table.
       *On it.*—Oil-lamp.
           Tantalus of two decanters.
    Grand piano.
       *On it.*—Shawl, oil-lamp, bowl of roses, 4 silver-framed photographs, ship ornament, 2 ornaments, loose music.
    Music rack.
       *In it.*—Bound copies of music.
    Duet piano-stool.
    Cabinet.
       *In it.*—16 ornaments.
       *On it.*—Small bust.
    Pedestal.
    *On it.*—Table-lamp.
    Small revolving bookcase.
       *In it.*—Books.
       *On it.*—Vase of roses, photographs.
    2 carpets.
    2 rugs.
    White bear-skin rug.
    Stair-carpet.

Standard oil-lamp.
Fender.
Fire-irons.
Pair of white net curtains.
Pair of heavy red curtains.
Curtain pole.
Heavy red curtain to back archway.
*On Mantelpiece.*—China clock.
  2 china vases.
  4 ornaments.
  Silver cigarette-box.
*Round Fireplace.*—11 miniatures.
*Above Fireplace.*—Oil-painting (portrait).
*Along Stair Wall.*—3 sporting prints.
*On Bookshelves.*—Books.
  Ornaments.
  Plants.
*In Conservatory.*—Table (not visible).

## ACT I

### SCENE 1

*On Stage.*—*On Tea-table.*—Silver tray with 2 cups, 2 saucers, silver kettle,
    teapot, milk-jug, sugar bowl, 2 plates, 2 teaspoons, 2 knives, jam-
    pot, pot with merkel, plate of bread and butter.
  Ashtray.
  Letter containing £5 note.
*On Serving-table.*—Tantalus of two decanters.
  Water-jug.
  6 tumblers.
  Cigarette-box.
  Ashtray.
  Bowl of roses.
*On Mantelpiece.*—Tall, slim vase containing single rose.
*In Work-table.*—Piece of embroidery, needle, skein of silks, thimble,
    scissors.
*On Bookshelves up* R.—Book.
*Off Stage* R.—Fishing-rod⎫
  Basket          ⎬(ABIGAIL).
  Shoes and socks ⎭
  Black bag containing 2 finger dressings, pair of scissors,⎫
    bottle of iodine, hypodermic syringe, small phial, packet ⎪
    of lint                                                   ⎬(SARCLET).
  Overcoat                                                    ⎪
  Pendant in case                                             ⎭
  Inverness (CASS).
*Off Stage* L.—Crust⎫
  Decanter (full)   ⎬(FLETTY).
*Personal.*—CASS.—Gloves, handkerchief.

### SCENE 2

*On Stage.*—*On Settee.*—HERDA's embroidery.
  Skein of silk.
*Off Stage* L.—Glass of whisky (SARCLET).
*At end of Act Strike.*—Bowl of roses from revolving bookcase.
  All dirty glasses.

## ACT II
### Scene 1

*On Stage.—Set.*—Tea-table between settee and chair c.
*By Serving-table.*—Watering-can.
    Pair of secateurs.
*On Revolving Bookcase.*—The " Lancet."
*On Conservatory Table.*—Bowl of roses from revolving bookcase.
*On Mantelpiece.*—Fresh rose in vase.
*Off Stage* R.—Towel (CASS).
    Basket (wild strawberries) (ABIGAIL).
*Off Stage* L.—Pile of linen⎫
    Punch-bowl and ladle  ⎬ (HERDA)
    Tray with 5 glasses (FLETTY).
*At end of Scene Strike.*—Punch-bowl.
    Tray.
    All dirty glasses.

### Scene 2

*On Stage.—On Work-table.*—HERDA's embroidery.
*Off Stage* L.—Cigar (SARCLET).
    Glass of milk (CASS).
*Personal.*—CASS.—Dead rose.

### Scene 3

*On Stage.—On Serving-table.*—2 tumblers.
*Off Stage* L.—Lamp⎫
    Portmanteau  ⎬(ABIGAIL).
    Lamp         ⎫
    Portmanteau ⎬(HERDA).
    Black bag ⎫
    Note       ⎬(SARCLET).

Any character costumes or wigs needed in the performance of this play can be hired from Charles H. Fox Ltd, 25 Shelton Street, London WC2H 9HX.

# SOUND EFFECTS

## ACT I

### SCENE 1

*Cue* 1.—*As* CURTAIN *rises.*
Fade in GULLS and SEA.

*Cue* 2.—After CURTAIN rise count four.
DOG barks twice.

*Cue* 3.—HERDA. " You haven't told me who it's from."
Fade out GULLS.

*Cue* 4.—ABIGAIL. " . . . from the splendour of his London Town."
Fade in GULLS.

*Cue* 5.—ABIGAIL. " Why are you so beautiful ? "
Sound of HORSE and CART approaching.

*Cue* 6.—ABIGAIL . . . *tears up the stairs.*
HORSE and CART stop.

*Cue* 7.—SARCLET *gently removes the cape from his shoulders.*
Sound of HORSE and CART going away.

*Cue* 8.—SARCLET. " Well, what do you think of it ? "
Fade out HORSE and CART.

*Cue* 9.—CASS. " You should be a painter, Edward, and live here always."
Fade out GULLS.

*Cue* 10.—CASS. " . . . and that she had a deep quiet laugh——"
Fade out SEA.

*Cue* 11.—CASS. " . . . crossing the park by the Serpentine . . ."
Fade in GULLS (*on the word* " Serpentine ").

*Cue* 12.—CASS. " . . . p'raps it's here ! "
Swell GULLS.

*Cue* 13.—CASS. " When I find it I shall be."
Fade GULLS.

*Cue* 14.—SARCLET. " Naturally I'm interested, Cassius. . . ."
Fade out GULLS.

*Cue* 15.—SARCLET. " . . . What are you talking about ? . . ."
Fade in SEA.

*Cue* 16.—ABIGAIL. " Yes——"
Fade in GULLS.

*Cue* 17.—CASS . . . *catches sight of the rose . . . on the mantelshelf.*
Fade out GULLS.

*Cue* 18.—ABIGAIL. " . . . she would know the feel of his hands and die ! "
Fade in GULLS.

*Cue* 19.—HERDA *puts the two coats over* FLETTY'S *arm.*
Fade GULLS.

*Cue* 20.—CASS *enters down the stairs.*
Fade out GULLS.

*Cue* 21.—HERDA. " . . . and the wind ! . . ."
Fade in GULLS.

*Cue* 22.—HERDA. " No, they're Weigs."
Swell GULLS.

*Cue* 23.—HERDA. " . . . is called in Island words—Blue Maa ! "
Fade in KITTIWAKES (Guy-Guy sound).

*Cue* 24.—HERDA. " . . . Look, that's the Tangie Maa . . ."
Fade out KITTIWAKES.

*Cue* 25.—CASS. " . . . you get a wish if you see your first goose. . . ."
Fade out GULLS.

*Cue* 26.—ABIGAIL. " *It is Skail.*" SARCLET . . . *is just about to speak* . . .
GONG.

82

SCENE 2
No cues.

ACT II
SCENE 1

*Cue 27.—As* CURTAIN *rises.*
Fade in GULLS.
*Cue 28.—*CASS *enters.* HERDA. " Good morning ! Sleep well ? "
Fade out GULLS.
*Cue 29.—*CASS. " . . . your tears and your roses, and your folded hands."
Fade in GULLS.
*Cue 30.—*SARCLET. " Exceedingly."
Swell GULLS : 1.
*Cue 31.—*SARCLET. " . . . I suffer from none of these things. . . ."
Swell GULLS : 2.
*Cue 32.—*SARCLET. " . . . I have been waiting for this."
Fade out GULLS.
*Cue 33.—*ABIGAIL. " . . . Miss Tanner had nine and her face was red and shiny."
Fade in GULLS and KITTIWAKES (Guy-Guy sound).
*Cue 34.—*ABIGAIL. " No ! She was an actress from London."
Swell GULLS and KITTIWAKES : 1.
*Cue 35.—*ABIGAIL. " Stephen would have liked Guy, wouldn't he, Herda?"
Swell GULLS and KITTIWAKES : 2.
*Cue 36.—*ABIGAIL. " . . . two years of rolling mists and sunshine."
Fade out GULLS and KITTIWAKES.
*Cue 37.—*SARCLET. " . . . I wish we'd gone to Longhope."
Fade in GULLS.
*Cue 38.—As* CURTAIN *falls.*
Fade out GULLS.

SCENE 2

*Cue 39.—*SARCLET. " That's Cass now." *As* CASS *opens the window.*
Fade in STORM.
*Cue 40.—*CASS *closes the window.*
Fade out STORM.
*Cue 41.—*HERDA. " That's Abigail ! " *As* ABIGAIL *opens the window.*
Fade in STORM.
*Cue 42.—As* ABIGAIL *closes the window.*
Fade out STORM.

SCENE 3

*Cue 43.—*After CURTAIN rise.
CLOCK strikes 4.
*Cue 44.—*CASS. " . . . and once I rang the bell too late ! "
Sound of HORSE and CART approaching.
*Cue 45.—*ABIGAIL *exits. After a pause.*
Sound of HORSE and CART going away.
*Cue 46.—*CASS. " Clisby ! Clisby ! This was what you wanted ! This was what you wanted ! "
Single note of laughter
*Cue 47.—*CASS. " . . . It's all over . . . rest . . . rest now . . . rest . . ."
Fade in GULLS.

# SIMPLIFIED LIGHTING PLOT

## ACT I

### SCENE 1

Daylight, late afternoon.
   Standard and table lamps out.
   Fire out.
   *Spot*—Chair c., settee, fireplace, piano, conservatory window.
   *Cue.*—CASS.  " . . . I can't write anything—nothing comes, nothing . . ."
   Start slow fade and continue to end of scene.

### SCENE 2

Evening.
   18 blue on sky.
   Standard and table-lamps on.
   Fire on.
   *Spot*—Chair c., settee, fireplace, piano, staircase.
*No Cues.*

## ACT II

### SCENE 1

Daylight, morning.
   Standard and table-lamps out.
   Fire out.
   *Spot*—Chair c., settee, fireplace, conservatory window, staircase, archway L.
*No Cues.*

### SCENE 2

Night.
   18 blue on sky (very dim).
   Standard and table-lamps on.
   Fire on.
   *Spot*—Chair c., settee, fireplace, piano, stairs.
*No Cues.*

### SCENE 3

Early morning, before dawn.
   18 blue and 60 grey on sky (very dim).
   Standard lamp on.
   Table-lamps out.
   Fire on (dim).
   *Spot*—Chair c.
*Cue 1.*—ABIGAIL *enters with lamp.*
   Bring in Spot on STAIRS.
*Cue 2.*—ABIGAIL *exits with lamp.*
   Fade Spot on STAIRS.
*Cue 3.*—HERDA *enters with lamp.*
   Bring in Spot on STAIRS.
*Cue 4.*—HERDA *exits with lamp.*
   Fade Spot on STAIRS.
*Cue 5.*—ABIGAIL *and* HERDA *enter with lamps*
   Bring in Spot on STAIRS.
   Bring in Spot on CONSERVATORY WINDOW.
*Cue 6.*—SARCLET *exits through the archway* L.
   Start slow build-up towards daylight lighting and continue to end of scene.

84

# INVENTORY OF WARDROBE

**CASS**

1 pair grey trousers.
1 dinner-jacket suit of velvet, brocade vest.
3 pairs white silk gloves.
3 pairs white kid gloves.
1 Inverness cape.
1 red silk handkerchief.
1 yellow scarf.
1 blue and red tie.
2 pairs black socks.
1 black dress tie.
2 dress shirts.
1 pair patent evening boots.
6 collars.
1 grey double-breasted jacket.

**SARCLET**

1 dress suit, 3 pieces.
1 silk waistcoat.
1 blue mixture lounge suit, 3 pieces.
1 grey tweed suit.
1 fawn waistcoat.
2 striped shirts.
2 dress collars.
2 soft white shirts.
4 dress shirts.
2 dress ties.
1 pair black evening boots
1 pair slippers.
3 dress studs.
1 overcoat, fur-lined.

**ABIGAIL**

2 blue skirts.
1 yellow evening dress.
1 brown skirt.
1 white dress, trimmed red.
1 check cloak.
2 white petticoats.
1 white blouse.
2 blue and pink check blouses.
1 pair black slippers.
1 pair yellow slippers.
1 red belt.
2 camisoles.

**HERDA**

1 tartan skirt.
1 rust blouse.
1 black dinner dress.
1 pink dress.
1 grey dress.
1 travelling coat.

2 white petticoats.
2 camisoles.
1 velvet belt.
1 pair black slippers.
1 hat, cream.

FLETTY

1 brown maid's dress.
2 aprons.
1 pair black shoes.
1 cap.